Sean Kachmarski

"Intriguing, absorbing, unashamed."
~ An avid cyclist and runner

"Compelling, entertaining, heart-warming."
~ A non-runner

"Inspiring, engrossing, captivating"
~ Marathoner and Outlaw Triathlete

"Inspirational, motivational and captivating"
~ Ultra Marathoner

"Just Finish! is self-deprecating, funny and brutally honest. It's about mind over matter, dogged determination, bloody mindedness and the kindness of strangers. It is the tale of the extraordinary lengths an ordinary man went to for the love of his family and became a local legend. Lengths achieved only because of the love and support of the family. It shows the human condition in its best light."

~ Alice Hearne

"As a back of the pack marathoner I can truly appreciate the emotions portrayed and felt the familiar spine tingle of endorphins when he crossed the line. Sean truly makes the marathon his own- a true champion and courageous marathon runner."

~ Julia Church

"Just Finish grabs the reader from the onset. It isn't a new story but it is told with honesty and heart. It is a story of highs and lows and getting back up on your feet and knowing you can do something and see it to the end."

~ VEK

First published in Great Britain as a softback original in 2019

Typeset in Baskerville

Design, typesetting and publishing by UK Book Publishing
www.ukbookpublishing.com

Edited and proofread by Paula Emery
www.proofitwithpaula.co.uk

Printed at Bluetree Group
www.bluetreegroup.co.uk

ISBN: 978-1-913179-18-2

Cover photo: © Marathon-Photos.com

Dedicated To:

My wife (Wendy) and kids (Ross and Tasha):
For their unwavering support and literal kicks out the door.

Parents, family and childhood friends:
Who still can't believe I am runner.

Rene and Leyla:
Well, you know what you endured!

PREFACE

The challenge of writing this book mirrored the challenges I had in learning how to run long distances as an adult. Both were journeys I never intended to be on, both had insurmountable obstacles I never thought I could navigate, and probably the most poignant, I had no experience in doing either. Without support from family, friends, professionals, and strangers my running journey, and this book, would never have happened.

All I can promise is that this story is true. My wife says I tend to speak in hyperbole, but, at its core, this is the story of a guy who decided to take his life back after a medical scare, the story of a guy who looked in the mirror and saw over 18 stone of wobbly jelly, the story of how a father tried to inspire his kids to stay active with mixed results, and the story of a man who set himself some challenges and how he achieved them. This story has some twists, turns, laughter, tears, successes, and failures. The story has been shared, in parts, with many people and most have suggested it should be written down and shared widely as it has inspired some to make changes within their own lives. Hearing such reactions has been very humbling and has inspired me to continue with running and to write this book.

To be honest, work, family and running doesn't allow me to read much, so I use Audible during my runs and commutes to and from work to get my daily dose of biographies, true crime, new concepts or theories, and self-help. It wasn't until I finished listening to *Finding Ultra* by Rich Roll, and *Fat Man to Green Man* and *Still Not Bionic*, both by Ira

Rainey, I realised I had a story that could be told. All three books were harrowing stories of unfit guys and how they became ultra-runners. Listening to these books, I noticed that, even though we were worlds apart geographically and physically, our journeys were similar. The main difference was that they were running sub 45-minute 10K races, sub 90-minute half marathons, and sub silly times for marathons. They were winning races, or at least placing in the top 10; they became lean and went on to run many ultras.

My story may not appeal to the elite runner, as there will be no mention of 6- to 8-minute miles, finishing in the top ten, or any Olympic qualifications. My story is more for the wannabe runner, the runner who is just starting out and the runner who feels more comfortable running 14- to 18-minute miles; the runner who will check the time of the previous year's race results to see what the slowest time was before they enter; the runner who has to phone the race organiser to see if there is a cut off time in the longer races; or the runner who will walk just out of view of the people at the finish, then turn on the jets for the last 100-metre sprint finish. All things I have done during my running journey (and still do).

Being a Canadian living in West Yorkshire, UK and starting to distance run at the ripe age of 44, came with the following challenges: being 18+ stone in weight, finding a work-family-run-life balance, and having no real concept of how to run long distances.

My earliest recollection of running comes from when I attended Saint Stephen's Junior High, in Calgary Alberta, Canada. Go Super Sonics! My first structured run was the dreaded compulsory 1K run from the gymnasium, around the block, back to the gym twice a week. It was ultimately a part of the Canadian physical education curriculum. Back in those days, and up to just four years ago, running would never be something I just did for fun; that would have been unthinkable!

At the time of writing this book, I have never broken 60 minutes for a 10K run, I run 5K comfortably in 39 minutes, I average 3 hours for my half marathons, and, frustratingly, I have never lost a ton of weight. I am the guy who comes last in almost every race, depending on the number of runners.

Now, if I am completely honest, I don't even like the physical act of running, but it's the feeling I get after a solid run that keeps me lacing up those shoes. The feeling is hard to explain but it's commonly known as a runner's high. I liken it to when Bradley Cooper's character takes NZT-48 in the movie *Limitless.* After any run, my sight, hearing and body confidence is heightened; I become acutely aware of my surroundings; I feel comfortable in my skin; and I feel invincible. The longer the run, the stronger the feeling. Now, couple that feeling with a sense of accomplishment and being a role model for my kids, it's clear that running was going to become part of my future.

I run for me, my family, anyone I secretly inspire and, of course, the medals. When I run a race or when I set myself a silly running challenge, I don't run to win, I just want to finish.

FORWORD

I don't even know the date; it was early January 2014, I think. It was a day like any other day and nothing out of the ordinary. I got up at 6:00am, washed, brushed my teeth, put my black George ASDA suit on, black socks, white shirt, black Doc Marten shoes with their yellow stitching, skipped breakfast, and was out the door by 6:30am to beat the traffic and arrive at my Leeds City Council desk by 6:57am. I did the same thing 5 days a week for 7 years. However, I had no idea that by the end of this particular day, I would be put on a path that would change my life.

After a regular day, during a regular drive home, from a regular job, the pain started. To start with, it felt like a runner's stitch, just under my rib on the left-hand side of my body. As an adult, I'd only ever got a stitch when I had to chase a receipt that had blown away by the wind in an Aldi car park. As a teenager, I got stitches a lot during daily American Football practices in high school playing left tackle, donning the number 52 for Bishop Grandin High School in the City of Calgary, in Alberta Canada. Go Ghosts!

There was no rapid breathing or lung expansion pressing down on my diaphragm, which is the actual cause of a stitch; I was only pulling off the M1 at junction 39. As I got closer to home the stitch turned into an ache. As I pulled up to our semi-detached house in Clayton West, the ache turned into a pain. A pain that seemed to get worse with every breath.

When I entered the house, instantly my wife Wendy said,

'What's wrong? You look pale.'

In between winces I replied, 'I don't know … I've had this pain in my side. It's been getting worse. I think I should go to the walk-in clinic.'

Wendy agreed, so that's what I did.

While grimacing with pain on each breath, I drove myself to the NHS walk-in clinic in Wakefield as the pain became intolerable. I parked, walked to the clinic, went up the stairs and into the packed waiting room. The small room was full of men, women and children sniffing, snivelling, chuntering, crying, sneezing, limping, bleeding, sleeping, standing, leaning and sitting on these heavily worn connected seats.

'Oh no … this isn't good,' I said under my breath.

I approached the counter and behind the glass barrier was a nurse who looked at me with this 'no chance pal' kind of look.

By this time, the pain had increased even further and I was holding my side like I had been stabbed.

'I would like to see a doctor please,' I pleaded.

'We're not taking any more patients today, I'm afraid', the nurse said with an empathic tone.

'Ummm, I have this pain … it's getting worse,' I begged.

She repeated, 'We're *not* taking any more patients today, I'm afraid.' This time she spoke with a sharper tone as if to say, 'Didn't you hear me the first time?'

I pleaded as my eyes started to well up, 'I am in real pain here … what do I need to do to see a doctor?'

'You can go to A&E. Shall I call you an ambulance?' she offered.

Now, even though I was in pain, I felt I was not in enough pain to warrant wasting people's time, so I said …

'No, that's OK. I can take myself to A&E.'

I left the waiting room in more pain than when I arrived. I was still shuddering with each breath and now had a bit of a limp. I was sort of hoping the nurse would see how much pain I was in and call me back to the desk. As I looked back with my best Canadian puppy dog eyes, I noticed she didn't even lift her head or give me a second thought.

In the car park, I now found myself wishing I had taken her up on the offer of an ambulance because I now had a 24-minute drive home and I wasn't sure if I could drive; stupidly, I went ahead and did it anyway. The pain was now affecting my breathing and I couldn't find a comfortable position. I barely made it home; I rolled out of the car and yelled for Wendy … no reply. I fell into the house, unable to speak as the pain was beyond tolerable.

'I NEED TO GO TO A&E!' I gasped … the only words I could muster, clutching my side with both hands.

In a panic, my wife sprang into action and called her mum to come and watch our son, Ross, who was 5 years old at the time. Even though Wendy's parents live only about 7 minutes away, it felt like hours before she arrived. When my mother-in-law got to the house, I was already in the car fighting the pain. At this point, it was as if a serrated dagger had been thrust into my side, just below my left rib. With each breath, it felt like somebody was whacking the end of it. There are only four things I remember during the 19-minute drive to Barnsley Hospital:

1. Seeing the panic in Wendy's face.
2. The two emergency stops Wendy had to make to avoid rear-ending cars as she kept looking at me to see if I was ok.
3. The pain being so intense it caused me to throw up. In the moment, I thought I would be clever and throw up into a novelty car trash bin Ross had got me for Christmas from the pound shop. What I didn't notice was the bottom was made of mesh, and both times I vomited, it seeped through onto my pants.
4. But most of all, I remember the pain…

Covered in vomit and tears, our arrival at the A&E department was a relief. Before Wendy could stop the car in front of the sliding glass doors entrance, I opened the car door and dashed to reception. I don't know what the distance was between the car door and reception … 10, 20, or 30 meters? All I know is that it was the longest run I had done in years, and, I can assure you, it was a personal best.

At the reception desk, I dropped to my knees and, by this time, could only talk in one-word sentences, 'Doctor … please.'

The nurse responded with a sense of urgency. She asked my name but I could only grunt. By this time, Wendy had parked the car and was able to fill in the mundane details. The nurse advised me to go to the waiting room. Waiting was not a word I wanted to hear. Upon entering the second waiting room of the day, I could see there were some empty chairs, and like in the movies, everyone turned their heads simultaneously to watch me fall into one of them squirming and groaning with pain. Within minutes, I heard my name.

'Sean? Sean Kalaminski?'

I looked up, and whispered to myself, 'Thank God.'

It didn't matter that they butchered my last name – most people do when they see it for the first time.

As I passed others who had been waiting for who knows how long, the only word I could find, I repeated three times. 'Sorry … sorry … sorry.'

Within minutes of my arrival, I was in a bed. A male nurse came into the room and asked,

'What happened?'

I continued to speak in only one-word sentences and tried to summarise the last 4 hours in eight words, 'Stitch, ache, pain, walk-in, busy, home, here, appendix?'

The nurse worked swiftly and attached some tubes to my arm while explaining everything he was doing, but I couldn't hear a word he said over my groans. The nurse left the room, but was soon replaced with Wendy. Then it happened. The pain stopped. All of a sudden, my vision was framed with frost like a window on a crisp Canadian winter morning and I sank into the most comfortable bed … ever. I looked at Wendy and said in a most peculiar way …

' Luv, you're the best. If you weren't married, I'd marry ya. Give me a smooch.'

Yes, the morphine had hit the blood stream.

Ironically, from that point forward, the pain never returned, ever. Not even to this day. Lying in bed with Wendy by my side, my thoughts turned to finding out what the hell happened. Other books would now regale you with the names of medical tests, procedures, and medical acronyms. I'm not going to do this; all I can say is that I was admitted to hospital for three days, in a room with at least six other people and my only barrier was a thin linen curtain that was drawn around my bed. As I was now feeling no pain, I didn't really know why I was there, nor did I want to stay and waste an NHS bed when I knew there was a shortage. I was just awaiting test results.

On the morning of the second day, I was called into a small room and shown an X-ray. It was explained to me that I had a kidney stone – actually – two kidney stones. One that was so big that it was still located at the centre of my kidney and was too big to pass, so it was staying put. The pain I had endured was the other pesky stone making its way through my left kidney; it was now in my bladder. I saw on the X-ray that it was just about to leave the bladder and enter the urethra. I was told I could not leave the hospital until it had passed. Now, on the x-ray, it looked small and I was told by the specialist it was much smaller than a grain of rice. In my mind, what *I* saw, was a large shard of glass that, at any moment, would enter my urethra and rip through my body via my penis. This was not something I was looking forward to.

For the next 10 hours, I was asked to drink lots of fluid and wee into a container, so they could analyse the urine to see if it had passed. With every bathroom break, I braced myself for the imaginary razorblades I thought would potentially shoot out of my penis when this stone passed. Luckily, this never happened. As Barnsley is a teaching hospital (and I guess my case was interesting), on the morning of day three I had to endure the eyes of six millennial medical students fixated on my exposed genitals, on what felt like an extraordinarily cold ward. Let's just say, I could not look any of those future doctors in the eye.

At midday, on day three, I guess my stone must have passed because the nurses started the discharge process. I was chomping at the bit to get home. By now, you might be asking, how did a kidney stone set me on the path to running? Well – it didn't. It was my subsequent condition that was found during all the poking, prodding, and extensive testing that prompted me to make a drastic change. A fatty liver? Now, that caught my attention.

I have a degree in Physical Education from the University of Lethbridge in Alberta, Canada. Go, Pronghorns! I once knew, specifically, what all the human organs did, their origin and insertion of all muscles, and how the body worked. I may have now forgotten most, if not all, of what I had learned, but one thing I do remember was that the liver was important.

My fatty liver was a non-alcoholic fatty liver, which was basically a build-up of fat within the liver itself and the liver cells. I deduced it was a non-alcoholic fatty liver because I didn't drink. Well, I do drink on limited occasions. My personal theory on drinking is this: I try to get from point A (sober) to point B (drunk) as fast as possible then try to maintain B as long as possible with a delicate balance of booze, water, and cola. In doing so, sometimes (most times), I would overshoot B and move onto C (the spins).

I am also known as a chick-drink drunk because I only drank sugary alcopops or, my favourite, shots of almost frozen peach schnapps. Now when I say limited, I mean very limited. I would probably try my drinking theory 1 to 2 times a year on a night out. I am not emphatically going to say that my formula for drinking didn't have an effect on my liver, maybe it did. I was thinking the cause was more my sedentary lifestyle, weekly takeaways, weekly secret visits to Mc Donald's, my 18 full-fat Cokes a week, plus bags and bags of my kryptonite Peanut M&Ms – what I like to call 'devil beans'.

As the doctor explained in our final chat, having high levels of fat in your liver was associated with an increased risk of problems, such as diabetes, heart attacks, and strokes. When spoken, those words hit me like a ton of bricks. I was 44, obese, and on the path to not seeing our son Ross graduate, walking our daughter Tasha down the aisle, or growing old with Wendy. Those shocking thoughts entered my mind at warp speed.

The doctor continued to explain my situation to me. I was in shock, but re-engaged in the conversation when the doctor said,

'The good news is, the liver is very resilient and can repair itself.'

The doctor tried to continue, but I cut him off.

'Doc?' I said, with a questioning, optimistic tone,

'Repair itself? How?'

MILE ONE

The True Beginning

A medical scare may have been the catalyst for change, but, on reflection, the true beginning started in cyber space. As this is a story of my running journey and not an auto-biography, here is the short version of how I ended up in England with my gorgeous wife and two fantastic kids.

In February of 2004, I was searching Match.com, and came across a short dark-haired beauty – her name was Wendy Ross. It was love at first sight; well, it must have been, as I moved to England and in with Wendy and her parents on 1st July 2004. We felt like naughty teenagers destined to be together, because we eloped on 12th August 2004. It was a whirlwind to say the least; a lot of cloak and dagger shenanigans took place during this time, which could surely fill the pages of another book.

When we got married, Wendy and I both joked that, as part of our wedding vows, this arrangement was only a 49-year marriage lease, which meant that, after 49 years of marriage, we could see other people. All kidding aside, Wendy routinely reminds me of this lease every wedding anniversary and has started some sort of countdown, which is weird.

After two years of being together, our first child was born. Ross Ronald Samuel Kachmarski arrived on 21st February 2006, followed by Tasha Abigail Kachmarski three years later, on 2nd June 2009.

Wendy and the kids have always been a driving force for me to achieve my goals; I hope I have done the same for them.

'Sean's health scare was a turning point for him. I didn't take much notice at the beginning when he said he was going to start running, but the running bug soon took hold. Sean's body isn't built like a typical runner; however, he has not been deterred and has remained focused, determined and resilient throughout. What he has achieved has been truly amazing, but, most importantly, his health has improved tenfold, which means he will be around for me and the kids for much longer now!

We are so very proud of Sean. He sets a good example for the kids about keeping fit and inspires them to do the same. It's not always been easy whilst Sean's been away on race days and the intense training involved, especially for the big races, but most of all, seeing Sean healthy in both body and, more importantly, his mental health, fills me with immense pride, awe and admiration.' ~ ***Wendy Kachmarski***

It was 10:00am on 26th September 2004 and I was channel surfing in my parents-in-law's granny flat, unemployed and with no real direction. I was sitting on our lumpy futon, eating Walkers crisps, sipping on 'full fat' Coke, in a pair of sweat-pants and a stained t-shirt. Just picture a fat, sweaty guy watching TV, picking crisp shards out of his clammy navel while balancing the remote on his extra-large spare tyre, and you will not be far off what it actually was like (or at least felt like). Wendy well and truly hit the jackpot with her Canadian prince charming.

My channel surfing came to rest on the 24th annual Great North Run on BBC One. I was transfixed. I got drawn into the stories, as with over 49,000 runners that year, there were many to be told. I watched the entire race. Watching people run was my first official running accomplishment. That year, the male winner was Dejene Berhanu from Ethiopia with a time of 59:37. With no concept of distance, time, or effort when it came to running a half marathon, I remember saying to myself 'not bad'. The top woman was Benita Johnson from Australia with a time of 1:07:55.

After the elite runners, it was time for the everyday grassroot runners of all shapes, sizes, and abilities. I vividly remember that it was at this point, when Wendy walked into the living room, that I said,

'Luv, I'm going to run this race next year.'

This remark actually made me chuckle out loud, which caused my stomach to jiggle.

2005, 2006, and 2007 all passed, and it became an annual joke that I was going to run the Great North Run the following year. Every year, in September, when I utter the famous words,

'Luv, I'm going to run this race next year.'

Wendy would reply with rolled eyes by saying,

'Yeah, right luv' in her thick Barnsley accent.

Back then, I could never have known that not only would I take part in the 2015 Great North Run, but it would be part of one of my first personal running challenges: three half marathons in three consecutive weekends.

MILE TWO

There IS an App for That

Following my stint in hospital, I was now home and on the road to recovery. As there was no more pain, my recovery was quick. It was very easy to slip back into my daily routine as if nothing had ever happened.

One particular day was like any other day; I was sitting on the couch eating Pringles and I was just about to open my second 750 litre bottle of full-fat Coke of the day. I was watching Star Trek: The Next Generation, specifically the Tin Man episode. It was an episode I had seen at least 10 times before and never liked. This time, I did have a job, a purpose, and a family. I was wearing shorts (not sweats) and a Nike jumper (not a t-shirt with stains). If you juxtapose this scene with the one in 2004 there were slight differences, but, in terms of my health, it was the same.

The words diabetes, heart attack, and stroke were still ringing in my ears and weighing heavily on my mind. A drastic change needed to happen, not just for me, but for my family. As I looked at the unopened bottle of Coke, something took hold. I'm not sure what it was, but it was powerful. Metaphorically, this bottle of Coke became everything I needed to change. In that moment, that bottle represented takeaways, sweets, cookies, cakes, fast food, and my kryptonite devil beans.

I walked to the kitchen in a trance, and rested my overhanging belly, which was peeking out of the bottom of my shrunken jumper, on the cold steel of the kitchen sink. I had been here before, trying to conjure up the will power to make the change that would literally save my life. It was as if the doctor was in the room, whispering in my ear because this became a huge moment, bigger than any other. I became the master of my own destiny and poured the bottle out as a symbolic gesture to myself; I was making a stand; I was drawing a line in the sand; and probably many other clichés. Just like that, I poured £1.25 worth of Coke down the drain and snapped back to reality; there were no trumpets; no arena filled with people cheering; and no 'ata boy' from anybody. Just me, standing at a sink, now thirsty for a Coke.

I had been a learning development officer for Leeds City Council for seven years at that time; it was my job to research, design, and facilitate training on topics such as change management, resilience, and well-being. I knew that, for any personal change process, using only will power was a bad idea. I needed to do three things: decide what I wanted to do, how I wanted to do it, and when I wanted to start. As a trainer, I always wanted to know the impact of my sessions and to measure impact you must have baseline data. Knowing all of this, I figured I would use the same logical framework in tackling what I wanted to do next.

Recording my weight and tracking would be the first thing I would do. So, without hesitation, the iPhone came out and the app store was opened. I started to search for the best weight loss tracker apps; there were many (free apps, 99p apps, £2.99 apps, and some at a whopping £10.99) After 45 minutes of searching and reading reviews, I found one just called Weight. It looked like the best one of the bunch, as it had colourful graphs and it logged weight and body fat percentages. I clicked 'get', paid 99p, and there it was, on my phone, waiting.

While scrolling, I noticed these C25K (Couch to 5 kilometre) and C210K (Couch to 10 kilometre) running apps. Thinking that walking was a good way to lose weight, the classic 10,000 steps per day popped into my head. Then it struck me, if walking helped you lose weight, then running would surely speed up the process (forgetting everything I learnt in university). I read how these C25K apps worked and thought I would give it a go. Once again, I clicked 'get', paid £1.99 this time, created a fitness folder on my iPhone, and moved both apps into it.

The next day, before work, I wanted to weigh myself to get that very important baseline data. I didn't bother taking off my house coat or pyjamas as I wanted it to be a big number. This was it; my journey started here. It was for my family, my kids, and my liver. I stood on the scales, looked down and saw 18st 3lbs, and recorded it in the app under Friday 28th February 2014. I then looked in the mirror and quietly said my personal mantra: 'Don't *think* you can ... *know* you can.'

MILE THREE

Crossing the Threshold and Losing Friends

After yet another regular workday, getting Ross to bed, ensuring Wendy was settled in watching Coronation Street, and checking in on Tasha to see if she was asleep, I washed the dishes left after tea, swept the kitchen floor, and got my work bag ready for the next day. In ensuring that all chores were done, and everyone in the house was settled, I was either subconsciously starting to train my brain to try and find that work-family-run balance, or it just might have been old-fashioned procrastination. It was now around 7:48pm and it was getting dark; it was time to start this journey. I needed to cross the threshold of the doorway.

It was a warm overcast night – warm enough for me to wear my Nike shorts – but I guess I was preparing for the worst, as I still wore a Nike shirt, Nike jumper, a light black bomber jacket, and, to top the outfit off, a pair of over-the-ear corded Sennheiser headphones. I walked to the corner of my darkening street, stood under the streetlamp that had just come on, and pressed Week One Day One on the C25K app. A short introduction included a 'Well done!' for taking my first steps to running 5K. The voice was male, so I quickly switched it to female as it was more soothing and easier to picture in yoga pants.

My first session started with a brisk five-minute walk to warm up. Then it alternated 60 seconds of running and 90 seconds of walking, for a total of 20 minutes. Following the five-minute cool down, the duration of my first night would only be a 30-minute session.

Because the first part of my route was downhill, instead of walking as instructed, I decided to start running prematurely to use the momentum of gravity and get rid of my nervous energy. This mistake started a chain reaction that got a bit out of control and put the session in jeopardy. While I was running, Sue then spoke via my headphones,

'Start running.'

(Sue is what I named my faceless trainer.)

The moment grabbed me because I was already running. As I hit the incline, my body shut down. I was now at the bottom of the hill, sweating profusely, red-faced, and desperate to get air into my lungs. I had only been running for 30 seconds. I gripped my shorts with both hands, bent over 45 degrees at the hips like I saw Michael Jordan do many times playing for the Chicago Bulls back in the day. I felt worthy to do that as I felt like an athlete again, much like I was in high school 26 years earlier.

Unfortunately, I had now muddled up the sequence and had to walk for two and a half minutes to catch up. I found each 60 seconds of running excruciating; I was running slowly, my legs ached, my lungs hurt, my heavy breathing made it look and feel like I was sprinting when I was probably actually doing a 21-minute mile. What I remember most about this first run was the sweat – my God the sweat! Out of the eight running intervals, I probably managed four. I started out way too fast, something that would stick with me later in my journey.

I had finished Week One Day One. I fell into the house like I did weeks ago with the kidney stone, but this time it was with what my wife would call a 'tomato face'. I got a 'Well done, luv!' from Wendy and then had the most glorious shower; a soothing hot steam shower for a job well done.

I reflected on the session when my head hit the pillow; because I knew I was going to do it all again tomorrow, there were a few things I needed to change. Just follow the app, don't start off too fast, wear fewer layers, and wear something reflective. Wearing all black at night didn't help the session or being seen by cars; it made me look like a cat burglar. This would be solved by a quick look on eBay.

Week One Day Two, Week One Day Three, and Four, and Five all passed. I stuck to my routine and fit the sessions in when I could. There were rest days, missed days, good sessions, and bad sessions. When it came down to it, I was still just doing what the app said while huffing and puffing and, of course, sweating. At this point, I still referred to my outings as sessions; they weren't really running, more like walking with a blip of running in the middle, much like a heartbeat rhythm you see on those machines on TV medical dramas such as Holby City or ER.

In 2014, not only did my running journey start, but there was a spike in my social networking usage. I had started using Facebook on 5th May 2007 and I created a YouTube channel called 'Sean Speaks' on 18th May 2012, essentially to keep in contact with my family and friends in Canada and my other friends around the world whom I'd met working and travelling. This was significant, because, for some deep-seated reason, I felt that my running had to be logged. I felt that if it wasn't logged it didn't count. This obsession later turned into my second personal mantra, 'If it's not on Strava, it never happened'. At this point in my journey, Strava was not a word I was familiar with. However, I did get overly comfortable using the 'share' function on my, now, antiquated Nike FuelBand and app.

The Nike FuelBand was good for the time and was the precursor to a Fitbit, or any other wearable tech used today. It tracked steps and converted your steps into fuel using some sort of secret Nike formula that also included height and weight. The FuelBand would link to an app via Bluetooth and showed limited graphs of your activity, duration, and effort. You could set a Fuel goal for each day, and I remember being chuffed with myself as I set it higher than usual the last couple of days and was achieving my 'GOAL' during every day that I did a session.

With this over eagerness to share every single detail of my sessions, I think my friends and family became fed up with my posts in their newsfeed. I say this because the number of my Facebook 'friends' went down by at least 10 during the first three months of me starting to run. I really didn't blame these 'unfrienders' as they were probably getting tired of my charts and graphs that had no relevance to anyone but me. Another reason for my reduction in virtual friends may have been due to my inane posts, which went like this:

'I thought the sliding door was going to open while running by a parked white van during tonight's run! It freaked me out! Watching too much Criminal Minds, methinks!' **#riskassessmentneeded**

Or,

'Dodging snails on sidewalk today, due to rain!' **#crushedit**

Pure nonsense.

Despite all this being said about my ridiculous running posts, what happened next was probably the most significant moment of my entire journey. One of my running updates got the attention of a friend I had not heard from in 11 years. A friend with whom I had worked aboard cruise ships while with Royal Caribbean International; a friend who lived over 10,500 miles away in Australia; a friend who pointed me in the direction of the marathon without me knowing it at the time – Briony Bullard. After not seeing each other for such a long time and not hearing from her for longer, she typed a reply to one of my posts, which set me on a course to achieving the impossible. She wrote just six words. 'Have you ever heard of parkrun?'

MILE 4

parkrun

Parkrun (with a small p), is a free 5K running event that takes place every Saturday morning in 20 countries across five continents. The first event launched was the Bushy parkrun, which was founded by Paul Sinton-Hewitt in 2004. It grew into a network of similar events called the UK Time Trials, before changing its name to parkrun in 2008. All you do is log on to parkrun.com, register, print out your barcode, search for the closest event near to where you live, show up on the Saturday at 9:00, run your 5K, scan your barcode to record your time, and then try and beat your personal best the following week. It's never a race against others, it's a race against yourself. I had never heard about parkrun until Briony mentioned it. Looking back, parkrun was a gateway into the running community, which, at the time, I was reluctant to walk through.

In reply to Briony's six words I posted, 'What's that?' She went on to explain what it was, with an unbridled enthusiasm that I could feel in her typed words. Notification after notification would pop up with more information about parkrun with the final post being a link to the Barnsley parkrun at Locke Park; at that time, it was the closest event to my house. This was weird as I didn't know Briony knew where I lived, specifically. She obviously did her homework – either that, or my long-time friend was a cyber stalker.

I wasn't sold on the idea as I was still only on Week 3 Day 4 on my app. Surely I needed to finish the app before I showed my 'tomato face in public? Plus, subconsciously I think I only ran at night so nobody would see me. It took some research, serious umming and ahhing, and some real self-reflection to convince me that parkrun would be a good idea. I registered and got my barcodes, but was that going to be it?

It was now Friday 14th March 2014 and the decision had to be made. Was I going to join the world of parkrun and daytime runners, or not? Four words popped back into my head and tipped the balance: diabetes, heart attack, and stroke. Just like that, a decision was made; YES, I was going to parkrun. Now, how could I make my decision a reality? Easy.

'I am going to my first parkrun tomorrow, what the hell has Briony got me into? #5KorBust' was posted on my Facebook feed.

Posting my intentions on Facebook and Twitter always seemed to make it harder for me to back out of something. Was it the guilt I would feel if I let my friends down? Probably not, as I am sure not many cared. Was it another type of Facebook guilt? I am sure there's a sociological experiment there somewhere.

Now that I had made my commitment to Briony publicly on Facebook and declared my intention to my other 410 friends who probably just scrolled right over my post, I sheepishly got my running gear ready in the corner of the room, told Wendy of my plan, then fell asleep wondering whether, when the time came, I could really do it.

The dreaded 7:30am came faster than I would have liked, being a Saturday. I usually had a bit of a lie in at the weekend. The internal angel and devil had a proverbial battle for the ages in my head.

Devil:
'Way too early, go back to bed!'
'Sean, you're never going to see this through, why start?
'Running? What the hell man? Get a grip!'

Angel:
'Diabetes.'
'Heart attack.'
'Stroke.'
Good, eventually, triumphed over evil.

I missed breakfast and changed into my running gear, which I thought would be practical and warm enough for an overcast day. I had my usual oversized Nike shorts, Nike t-shirt, Nike sweater, and tuque, or beanie. Plus, my newly bought Altura waterproof reflective yellow cycling jacket. With my over-the-ear leather Sennheiser headphones, iPod, space-aged looking Nike 'Boing' shoes, Nike FuelBand, and my laminated barcode, I thought my ensemble was complete. Looking back, the outfit may have been OTT, but you can judge for yourself as I captured my first parkrun experience as a special episode of my YouTube show and this can be viewed if you search YouTube for 'Sean's 1st parkrun.'

This picture was snapped at Locke Park on Saturday 15th March 2014, my very first parkrun. I had my own unique look and fashion sense!

I arrived early as I did for everything; on this occasion, it was so that I could get my bearings and not look like, what my son would call, a newb. Well, looking at what other people were wearing, I might as well have had a bright flashing sign around my neck that said 'Newb'. There were no over-the-ear headphones, no Nike 'boing' shoes, and no three layers. All I saw were spandex tight pants, running group t-shirts, and a sea of neon. I felt like a proverbial fish out of water.

I embarrassedly went to the first timers briefing as I saw it as, yet, another way to attract attention to myself. I was told the rules: three times around, stay to the right so the fast runners could pass, be sure to have your barcode for the end (no barcode – no time). Then the words were uttered that would allow me to relax a bit: 'Remember … it's not a race, it's a run.'

Looking back, the vulnerability I felt was completely unwarranted; the smiles, the banter I overheard between runners, the worried, impatient, and hungover looks of runners of different shapes, ages, sizes, and abilities, was weirdly calming.

I had made it this far and I needed to do this for me, so I entered what I like to call a 'focus bubble'. This is an abstract transparent bubble that kept all sounds, emotions, sights, and distractions out. This allowed me to focus on what I needed to do to finish. Entering my bubble is quite easy; all I need to do is tune into my loud dance club mixes with mega bass.

I started at the back as I knew I would end up there eventually and didn't mix with anybody, which was a newb mistake on my part. I really missed an opportunity to mix with likeminded people who just wanted to get around in one piece. This is a mistake I continue to make as I still prefer to run by myself.

The air horn blew; I started a new activity on my Nike FuelBand; and off I went. With 204 runners on this day, I felt that first boost of adrenalin that only a race could give you. On setting off, I started passing people as the moment took over. The moment soon passed as the incline of the starting hill took hold of my legs, knocking the wind right out of me in the first minute, forcing me to walk (it's a run, not a race). Due to starting off too fast, the people I passed were now overtaking me. While crossing the apex of the first hill I took advantage of gravity and started running, but the decline soon ended and so did my running. 'Tomato Face' was in the building and I had only been running, well slogging, for 5 minutes.

It was at this point I was longing for my downhill night-time runs and I was seriously contemplating going home. I was only half a mile in and at a point where there was a fork in the path. I could take the right fork to where my car was parked (and was probably still warm) or I could take the left where there was a hill that can only be described as WTF?!

I think it was the fact that there were still people around me and I didn't want to look any more of a fool than I already felt that made me take the high road, or should I say, the steep path. This hill was a beast; it did flatten out but it was then followed by the beast's older and steeper brother. At this point, there was nobody around, but I had gone too far to return to the car, so up the hill I walked. It was at the top of the hill that I remembered what was said at the newbie briefing, 'three times around'. This meant I would have to do these hills two more times. My legs and lungs were burning, and I remember thinking, 'Thanks Briony; I thought we were friends.'

I had finished the first lap and got the obligatory, 'Keep going!' 'Well done!' and 'You're almost there!' from the well-wishers and parkrun volunteers. They were all congregated around the finish line waiting for the first runner to cross the line. It would take me two more times around to be worthy enough to enter the finishing funnel.

Once I passed the finish for the first time, I was once again at the crossroads; car or beast. For my sins I chose the beast again, which was a moral victory as nobody would have known, I could have got in my car never to be seen at Locke Park again. It was either the Facebook guilt I would have felt or the fact I was halfway to finishing my first parkrun that made me slog up the hill for a second time.

I made it to the start area again; this time, there were louder cheers, but not for me. Cruelly people were dashing pass me on the left at top speed, they were doing their sprint finish and entering the finishing funnel to their delight. I was clearly last and I still had one more lap to go. As it was my first time, I did wonder whether they would wait for me to finish.

Psychologically, the third time around was relatively easier; all I was thinking was, one more time up that bastard hill and I'm done. I very slowly walked up the never-ending hill, to save my energy for the downhill sprint finish. Physically, it was a painful grind that I wasn't sure I ever wanted to repeat. My body was spent, mucus stringing from my bottom lip due to breathing so hard, sweat stinging my eyes, lungs exploding, and muscles aching as I crossed the line and subsequently collapsed on the grass once my barcode was scanned.

It was done; my first parkrun. I was relieved, happy and impressed with myself. Somewhere between thinking my lungs were going to pop out of my chest and waiting for my pulse to return to normal, a sense of accomplishment filled the air. I said thanks to the volunteers and returned to my now cold car.

Within an hour, I got the email with my first parkrun result:

'2014-03-15 Barnsley parkrun results for event #164. Your time was 00:41:48.

Congratulations on completing your 1st parkrun and your 1st at Barnsley parkrun today. You finished in 204th place out of a field of 205 parkrunners. Well done on your first run. We have set this as your PB.'

Just for the record, the 205th place was a parkrun volunteer whose job was to ensure everybody finished, by walking behind the last runner. At the end of the day, a 5K baseline had been set. Now the question was, would I return to see if I could beat it?

After my first parkrun experience, the C25K app was no longer used. At the time, I likened the cost of purchasing the app to buying a coke and a bag of crisps. Reflecting on it, the app was probably one of the first investments in my journey, an investment that may have paid dividends health and fitness wise, but it did lead me down a money hole of gadgets, clothing, and other running bric-a-brac.

For the following weeks, all I did was a two-mile loop from my house, using my Nike FuelBand for timing, but mostly using it to accumulate Fuel points, later to be shared on Facebook once synced. I went out slogging pretty much every second day, walking more than I was running. Then the Friday decision was in front of me. To parkrun or not to parkrun, that would be the question.

It was Saturday 22nd March 2014 and I was at the start line of my second parkrun. This time, the four layers were replaced by just two. I started at the back, attacked the beast three times and finished at the back. Once again, within the hour, I got the official results via email. I waited intently to see if I had beaten last weeks' time.

'2014-03-22 Barnsley parkrun results for event #165. Your time was 00:39:26.

Congratulations on completing your 2nd parkrun and your 2nd at Barnsley parkrun today. You finished in 169th out of a field of 176 parkrunners. Congratulations on setting a new Personal Best at this event! Congratulations on your fastest time this year.'

Firstly, new PB, YA! Secondly, not last? Wow!

The days between Saturdays became shorter as my thoughts were about beating my weekly parkrun time. On 29th March 2014, I was, yet again, at the start of another parkrun, my 3rd in three weeks. This time, my over-the-ear headphones were replaced with inner-ear sport earbuds, my Nike 'Boing' shoes were replaced by new Nike Lunar shoes from Junction 32's Nike Clearance store. This was only due to an internet review of Nike 'Boing' shoes that showed they were prone to turning ankles. They looked cool, but were not practical for running.

Once again, I started at the back of the pack, attacked the beast three times and finished at the back of the pack. At this point, the results email became a highlight of the week (sad, I know).

It did take me 25 parkruns to realise that I could just ask what my time was as I passed the finish line. Plus, I did self-time and knew my approximate finish time, but there was something more satisfying about getting the official result.

With this being said, my result email arrived, as usual, within the hour.

2014-03-29 Barnsley parkrun results for event #166. Your time was 00:37:56.

Congratulations on completing your 3rd parkrun and your 3rd at Barnsley parkrun today. You finished in 153rd place out of a field of 161 parkrunners. Congratulations on setting a new Personal Best at this event! Congratulations on your fastest time this year.'

At the writing of this book I have completed 66 parkruns. It has taken me over four years to do them. I even captured the milestone of my 50th run as part of my YouTube show, Sean Speaks (search 'Sean's 50th parkrun').

As 50 is a parkrun milestone, you got a free red shirt with a 50 on the back. I got mine in the mail, quickly tried it on, but it was too damn small. I didn't realise at the time that this would foreshadow the fact that 99% of the shirts I earned through my blood, sweat, and tears from running would never fit, even though they were XXL. In 2019, the parkrun people did away with the shirts and now give out lapel pins, which are kind of cool. I long for the day when I get my 100-parkrun pin, and I can wear it on my suit on special occasions. The 250-parkrun pin would be even better; one might say 'epic', maybe someday.

My current parkrun PB is 00:32:24, which was achieved on my 58th parkrun on 15th July 2017. This parkrun PB remains to this day. The beast has never allowed me to break that 5K 30-minute barrier at Locke Park, but I am determined to do it at some point.

Parkrun has been interwoven into the fabric of my running journey and the beast has kept me grounded. Parkrun also made me believe that I was a runner. People may look to famous runners for inspiration; I remember learning at school about Abebe Bikila from Ethiopia, who ran long distances barefoot. Paula Radcliffe or Mo Farah from Great Britain were famous for their Olympic journeys, and, from Africa, the legend Haile Gebrselassie and his many accomplishments.

For me, it's the people that I eventually met at parkrun whom I consider my true running heroes. Julia Church, David Lee, Leyla Brooke, Christopher Walker, Jon Gratton, Shelia O'Carroll, Tracy Hughes, Hayley Stinchon, Rachel Norton-Warsop, and, even though we did not meet at parkrun, Briony Bullard. It is for this reason that their stories are intertwined with mine.

'I was introduced to Sean on social media by my running buddy Briony, who happened to work with Sean on board cruise ships years ago.

They say it's a small world and it is – especially since I now live in Australia! But Sean attends my hometown parkrun in Barnsley! I began following his running journey because we were similarly paced runners and had a couple of things in common.

I was lucky enough to run with Sean in Barnsley, when I was home visiting family. It was a great morning. Talking to someone you have never met, but feel like you've known them for years is a funny but heart-warming feeling.

Sean loves a challenge and he has often set huge targets, which may be a little hair-brained, but he always pushes through and gets them done. ***~ Julia Church***

***

During her visit from Australia, and as part of a future running challenge, Julia Church and I met up at her old stomping ground, Locke Park for yet another parkrun.

I know Sean because we live nearby and have children of a similar age. His daughter and my son were in the same class at nursery and into first school. I always ran a bit, particularly before I had children.

One day, when I hadn't run for quite some months, I saw Sean at school picking up his daughter, wearing a parkrun jacket. I'd heard of parkrun, but didn't know much about it. He told me what it was all about, and encouraged me to go along to the next one local to us (Barnsley).

I turned up the following Saturday in the freezing cold - it was February! Sean greeted me like an old friend, not a passing acquaintance, and made me feel much better about being there. I really struggled with that first parkrun, and was last. What will stay with me forever is that Sean was waiting for me at the finish. Parkrun has a brilliant, supportive ethos anyway, but for someone who barely knew me, but who I know has been unfit and panting like me, and has to fit exercise and sport around the demands of a young family and a full-time job, was just fabulous. Thank you for that Sean.

As time has gone on, I have more time for my first love of cycling, but I try and run too to stay fit and strong enough to enjoy the bike. Now I go to the Junior parkrun with my children; at age 7 and 10, they are both faster than me. I like to think I am built for distance rather than speed!

I love following Sean's Facebook blog and his self-imposed challenges. I like his raw honesty and his resilience. He inspires me that ordinary folk can meet these challenges. It always lifts my spirits to see him pounding the local roads in his Maple Leaf hat. Once or twice I haven't recognised him, he had lost so much weight. He's keeping it real, and just showing most of us all that we have no real reason not to get up, get out, and get fit. ***~ Alice Cooper***

****

'I regularly saw this guy run past my large bay window in the village and I thought I recognised him. My son confirmed he was his friend's dad, Sean. It seemed that day in, day out, he'd pass by in his running gear; I admired his determination.

It was around this time that I was in a lull. I'd worked hard over the past few years to lose my baby weight, then I hit a brick wall. My health had deteriorated over the previous twelve months and I was cursed with relentless migraines and my weight crept back up. I felt the hard work I had put in years before, building up my running and following the C25K programme; Sean motivated me to keep going' **~ *Hayley Stinchon***

***

Statements such as these made in public, and in private, made me believe I could do so much more. It's what happened next that not only amazed my friends and family, but brought me to tears, not once, not twice, but many times.

MILE 5

Running Naked?

Early in my journey I realised that, to be successful, I essentially had to teach myself how to run. I had to learn the best way to run up hill (use my arms and stay on the balls of my feet), downhill (use longer strides), and find out what the hell fartlek was (periods of fast running intermixed with periods of slower running). YouTube was great, books were ok, but I found magazines the best way to learn how to run and learn this new language. There was one magazine that I kept buying at the news stand: Men's Running Magazine. It was very informative on many levels.

Eventually, to save money, I subscribed and received the newest copy each month through the post, instead of looking for it at the corner store. Over the years, I did get my picture on the 'My Race Face' page and, in 2015, my 'Question for the Expert' email that I sent was published on their 'letters' page, winning me a Gore windproof running shirt.

In a recent copy, I came across the term 'running naked'. It means to run with no technology. Just run, outside, inside, and enjoy it, with nothing on which to log that you have just put in some hard-earned miles. As my mind tried to comprehend running without any technology, I thought if running naked was running with only a t-shirt, shorts and a pair of shoes, and this was to be the norm, metaphorically, with all the tech I was using, I was wearing a tuxedo, with a white shirt, bow tie, waist coat, cummerbund, wing-tipped shoes, a top hat, white gloves, and a monocle.

For some of my runs, the amount of technology I was wearing was laughable. During one parkrun, I had two heart rate monitors strapped across my chest; they were both measuring the same thing, but I foolishly wanted to see if they were consistent measurements. One was synced to my Polar watch and one was synced to my iPod, which was ultimately synced to an app. I also had some sports headphones to listen to music and a Nike+ Pod in my shoe to measure my pace, synced to yet another app on my phone. Let's just say that it was a nightmare; the straps for my heart rate monitors kept coming undone, and as they were under my Nike compression top, they were not easy to get to and fix. My wireless headphones kept dropping my music, I think due to the number of apps I was using. Also, my iPod ran out of charge before I finished. A perfect storm of technological disasters, which, in the end, made me look like Star Trek's Locutus of Borg, with all these wires and straps coming out from who knows where.

Heart rate (average, resting, and highest), steps, distance, pace, average pace, calories, speed, average speed, cadence, elevation, Vo2 Max, stride length, and weight were just some of the measurements I obsessed over. I would measure the amount of sweat produced if I could. With this being said, and with all this information captured, I had no idea what most of the measurements meant, I just had this information at hand if anyone asked. To this day, nobody has ever asked.

I am not one to give advice; however, if I can save anyone from making the same mistakes that I did, I would feel that I have made a difference. This is my advice to any other gadget geeks who are considering taking up running; save your money for the best tech, don't work your way up the ladder of cheap tech tat like I did.

I started out with the Nike FuelBand, which was my first wearable tech, and it suited the needs I had at the time. I then bought the cheapest Polar watch and heart rate strap as I wanted to track my heart rate. It was ok, but the watch was small, and I could not see the face well enough to see the stats while running. I then found what I thought was the best buy ever: a Nike running watch. Brilliant right? I then had to buy several accessories to track my heart rate and pace (heart rate strap, heart rate monitor, and a Nike+ Pod Kit). It, once again, suited a purpose but didn't track enough stats. Next, the TomTom Runner watch: it actually tracked my heart rate with no chest strap, so I had to have it and I got it cheap. I realised why it was so cheap when TomTom released the TomTom Runner 2 a month after I had just bought the Runner 1. Thanks to a quick sale on eBay, I was able to buy the TomTom Runner 2.

In the end, I finally ended up shelling out more money for the Garmin Forerunner 235, which is a mid-range Garmin product. This wearable tech does everything my past buys did and so much more. In three years I probably spent enough money on tech tat too buy two, if not three, Garmin Forerunner 235s. There are many other brands of top-of-the-line wearable running tech out there, so save your money up and buy the top tech instead of doing what I did. Remember, this was just the cost of the watches I wore compared to the copious amount of other running tech I have used; don't get me started on sporting headphones. Also, what I found was, if you buy top tech they last longer; I am on my 3rd year using the same tech, but I do have my eye on the Garmin Forerunner 645. Don't tell my wife.

My running tech of course had to sync to something … enter Strava. Strava gave me real-time stats about how much effort I had put in each and every run; it allowed me to add the obligatory running selfie; and, of course, it had a share function. So, the phrase, 'If it's not on Strava, it never happened' was born. There had been days when I had gone out for a 1 to 3 mile run and didn't notice a low battery that stopped mid run, or I had forgotten to press the button enough to start the watch. In these cases, I re-ran these miles once the tech was sorted as if the first run never took place. I always felt guilty manually adding the run, as it felt like cheating, plus you never got the cool GPS map if you added a run manually.

So, running naked is not for me, but as running has given me a lot of body confidence, I may just do one of the British Naturism-hosted 5K and 10K runs at their annual NudeFest in Somerset!

Before contemplating anything like that, there was one race I had to conquer. It was now nearing the end of 2014 and I had a few miles under my belt, so it was time to utter those ridiculous words …

MILE 6

'Luv, I'm Going to Run the Great North Run Next Year!'

The first Great North Run was held on 28th June 1981 with 12,000 participants. By 2011, the number of participants had grown to 54,000. In 2014, there was 56,000 runners, so I had no idea what the number would be in 2015. Most of my running friends were on their 3rd, 4th, or 10th Great North Run.

In December 2014, I recited the now famous and ludicrous words I had said every year for 11 years. This time, they were not just hollow words. I had set up an email reminder service to let me know when the entries would be open for the 2015 event.

Email received 6th December 2014.

'Thank you for signing up to the reminder service for the following event(s):

Great North Run 2015

When the event(s) open for entries, we will send a reminder email:'

At this point in my journey, I was increasing my weekly and daily mileage to about 12 to 15 miles a week, not because I had to, because

I could. The feeling after a good run was still intoxicating and I soon realised that the longer the run was, the bigger the rush. The chemicals that were released when I ran – endorphins, dopamine, or serotonin – continued to make me feel invincible and I wanted more.

The idea of running a half marathon was still a bit of a pipe dream; I had to get in through a lottery system. If I am honest, a small part of me didn't really think I was going to get in anyway, and if I was being really, really honest, a big part of me didn't even think I could run that distance. But, if I entered the lottery and failed, I would be at least seen as giving it a go. There was also a small part of me that was saying, if I was ever going to run the Great North Run, it should be now because I was already running.

The reminder service worked like a charm, letting me know I could enter on 3rd January 2015.

On that day, I entered with reckless abandon; I filled out the entry form, ticked the XXL finishing t-shirt box, paid the money, and clicked send. I did hesitate before I clicked send because I was still struggling with my 5K parkruns and didn't really think I was ready, even if I got a spot. I decided to leave it to fate and clicked send anyway.

Email received 3rd January 2015:

'Dear Sean Kachmarski

Congratulations. You are now registered in the Daily Mirror ballot for the Great North Run 2015 and stand a chance of joining 56,999 others on the start line of the world's greatest half marathon.

Good luck!'

Now we wait.

The waiting didn't really take that long, as on 11th February 2015 an email landed in my inbox with the subject heading 'Your general ballot results'. I could not believe it, this was it!

Email received 11th February 2015:

'Congratulations!

You have been successful in the general entry ballot and have secured your place in the 2015 Morrisons Great North Run.

We look forward to seeing you on the start line on Sunday 13th September!'

Talk about shit getting real – this shit was in UHD.

MILE 7

Great North Run Prep

From then on, 2015 was basically filled with parkruns and local training sessions in an attempt to better my parkrun time. From March 2014 to March 2015 I had run 27 parkruns out of a potential 52. I was now running more than I walked and there were days my legs felt brilliant and I just kept running. I would finish some runs and look at my watch and it would say 4 or 5 miles. After a routine run, I found out the distance from my house in Clayton West to the Denby Dale Train Station and back, was 6.2 miles or 10K. I paused for a moment and tried to comprehend the fact I had just run 10K for the hell of it. This revelation knocked the wind out of me more than the run itself. It took me 01:41:32, but I was in shock, and if it was not recorded I would not have believed it. A 10K run for so-called fun? Who would have thought it?

All these miles were great prep for the big day, but I needed practice running with others. Not just the almost 200 people at parkrun, but 1000s of people. So, it was time to enter an official race. The 2015 Hospice Wakefield 10K run was on 29th March and some of my friends had asked if I was going to run in it. Even though it was an epic challenge, I considered accepting the test of my first official 10K race.

A friend shared the race link on my timeline on Facebook and I had a quick look as I didn't want to set myself up to fail. The first thing I looked at was the running time of the slowest runner in 2014, which was 02:04:04. This meant I might not be last as I knew I could run a 10K in under 2 hours. I then looked at the number of runners. It was 1,344, which was enough for my first big race. I then checked the elevation; I hated hills. I know hate is a strong word but, I really despised hills. Fortunately, it turned out to be flat. But, there was one rule that turned me off this race; no headphones were allowed. This would mean no 90s club remixes pounding in my ears as I pounded the pavement. This was a deal breaker; I needed my music and I wasn't willing to give up *Ride on Time* by Black Box for anybody. So, at that point, I decided to pass on the Wakefield 10K.

A few days passed, but I couldn't ignore the fact that this Great North Run prep opportunity was too important to dismiss. I took it upon myself to have a closer look at this 'No headphones' malarkey. I posted a question on the Wakefield 10K race Facebook page, 'How strict are they with this ban on headphones?' I got several replies; some were useful and some weren't, but the message was basically the same.

'It is for the runner's safety that there are no headphones allowed; most of the race is on a closed road but we want runners to be able to hear any potential traffic, marshal instructions, and emergency services if warranted.'

I weighed up the idea of some much-needed race day prep, versus the headphone embargo. In the end, I felt I should bite the bullet and enter. I entered just under the wire for them to mail me my number and was now committed, once again, to feeling vulnerable. This time, I didn't have my music to hide behind or motivate me. My focus bubble was going to be thin and I didn't know what I would do if it popped.

Getting a race number in the mail always excites me. This time, I wasn't sure whether it was because I was in disbelief that I was at a place in my life at which I was actually entering a race, or because I was a part of something bigger. Number 206 arrived a week before the Wakefield 10K, and, as always, at the forefront of my mind was whether or not I would actually finish.

My training for the race meant that my weekly mileage increased. I was probably doing 12 to 16 miles a week at this stage, mixing my runs with hills and speed work. My tech was sorted for the race: TomTom Runner 2 and my phone for selfies and sharing. The only thing missing was my iPod Nano and my new sports sweatproof headphones (damn you, health and safety). The only thing now to get sorted was my look; what was I going to wear so I didn't look like a newb? I bought a pair of Nike running dri-FIT running pants. These tights, made of part polyester and part spandex pants, seemed to be a runner's standard attire. However, I was not confident enough to wear such tight pants on their own, so I wore my standard baggy Nike shorts over them. I selected what I thought was a cool and practical shirt. I had ordered a Canadian cycling jersey from eBay, which had three pockets at the back for any running items I might need. It was tight but comfortable. Under this shirt, I had my standard short sleeved Nike compression shirt, which, in such a tight shirt, I found useful for hiding and controlling my wobbling belly.

So, everything was set; it was now the night before the race and my pre-race routine was born. Pasta, of course. Everybody knows you eat pasta before you race. Also, I was so proud of my running outfit I set it out on the floor with my number and took a picture and posted it on Facebook. I later found out that this was not something I started, it was something that most people in the running community did. Once again, I felt like a newb!

On Sunday 29th March 2015, I was up early and had my breakfast: oatmeal, toast, banana, multivitamin, and an effervescent tablet with vitamin C + zinc dissolved in water. My family was still asleep, so I crept out the door at 7:00am for a 9:00am race start. With a quick stop at Tesco Express on Wakefield Road for some water and a Twix to scarf down just before the race, I was on my way to Wakefield City Centre.

The 22-minute drive went quickly. That could have been the excitement, the empty Sunday roads, or it could have been songs such as Run to You by Rage, or Ray of Light by Madonna, which I had turned up loud in the car. I tried to absorb the music I knew I would be running without.

Being early has its advantages; the car park is never full, you can get your bearings as to the location of the start line, the finish line, the toilets, and the first aid tents. Being early also has its disadvantages; I had 90 minutes to kill. There were other like-minded early birds, but they were prepared either in makeshift bin bag shirts or wrapped like a baked potato in their tin foil blankets. I made a mental note of everything.

The local DJ was playing music and the sponsor and retail tents were filling fast. I could actually feel the nervous anticipation building; it was overwhelming and a bit emotional. I was just about to run 10K with an official number and with other people and the only thing that made me stand out, was the huge Canadian maple leaf on my chest.

It was 8:30am and we were asked to make our way to the starting funnel. Being early, I was already at the start of the funnel where I noticed these times on giant placards: sub 30 mins, sub 40 minutes, sub 50 minutes, and so on. Almost as a reflex, I walked to the back of the pack; I stopped at the sub 90 minutes placard and waited. Eventually, I was surrounded by neon and spandex and we were trapped like cattle. I was well and truly in my 'focus bubble', unaware of my surroundings and laser-focused on the task at hand. Then it happened; I caught a glimpse of something that instantaneously popped my bubble and I was now fully aware of my surroundings. I was livid and became increasingly enraged as I noticed I was surrounded by people with headphones. Health and safety my ass! It seemed like everyone had them on; on reflection, it was probably only 40% of the people around me that were listening to something. The rest were taking their start-of-race selfies and posting them on their favourite social networking sites. After a quick chunter under my breath and a major mental note, I re-entered my focus bubble.

Hurry up and wait seemed to be the feeling in the air, but I was just waiting for the starting horn. The race finally started, and our slow-moving caravan moved toward the metal starting gantry. I pressed the buttons on my GPS watch, checked it twice to see if it had started and off I went. There were many more people than there ever was at my local parkrun. People were stopping to re-lace their shoes; they can't have seen them come undone with all of the excitement. There were people in fancy dress, people holding hands in unity for their charity, walkers, and others who looked as determined as I was. At this point, I was bobbing and weaving to find a space to settle into my regular pace. As standard, I started passing people and set off way too fast. I eventually settled in and found my rhythm. As this was my first run without music, all I could hear was very heavy breathing and my shoes striking the asphalt.

The route was undulating but not severe. It was like a child's roller-coaster going up then down, up then down. I could feel the strain in my legs a bit on the uphill and always welcomed the following down hills. I would pass people then others would pass me. I stuck my head out of my focus bubble just a few times to embrace the life blood of any race – the cheering volunteers, the marshals, and the well-wishers. The supporter's handmade signs, cheers, and high fives from kids were like a wave of energy pulsating through me, even though from their perspective, it was probably like watching the worst parade ever.

At the halfway point I looked at my watch to see that I smashed my parkrun 5K personal best by just over 1 minute; my watch read 00:32:10. I was motoring and felt good. I grabbed some water on the run as it was on a bit of a downhill and I didn't want to walk and lose momentum. It was an out and back, which meant you started from point A, hit point B and came back the same route back to point A. This also meant I would see all the people I was in front of. I saw that there were a few behind, and, at this point, I knew I would not be one of the last three runners like I usually was at Locke Park.

I started to feel the strain in my legs and my pace slowed; people were passing me as I hit, what I felt was, a mini wall. Starting off too fast had caught up with me, AGAIN! I really slogged through miles 4 and 5. I wanted to stop and walk, but didn't. I was now running a 15-minute mile and getting slower. I eventually saw the five-mile sign and felt a shot of adrenalin because I knew there was only one mile left; I pictured myself with one mile to go at my local parkrun. One more time up the beast and then it's all downhill from there, I thought. I increased my pace and started passing others. The finish was getting closer and I started to slow again, not because I was tire, but because I was saving my energy for the famous Kachmarski sprint finish in front of all the people at the end. I caught sight of the glorious finishing gantry and turned on the jets and as I passed people, the crowd cheered louder. My lungs were bursting, my legs felt like stumps, but I crossed the finish line with a time of 01:12:23. Brilliant!

I collected my goody bag, my medal, and my XXL shirt that I'd pre-ordered when I entered the race. The efficiency of the race organisers surprised me, as I received a text with my results as I limped back to my car. It stated that I had finished the Wakefield 10K in 01:10:10. My pleasant feeling of shock turned to confusion; I had two different times here. What's this gun time and chip time? I was too exhausted to care at this point; I just wanted a hot shower. I sat in my car, rifled through my goody bag, scarfed down the standard race Mars Bar, took the habitual end-of-run selfie with my medal, posted it on Facebook along with **#survived**, then drove home.

I left behind all the excitement of the race day finish, the sounds from the racing village exuberance, and the opportunity to meet others who may have been on the same journey. Looking back, it was sad that I didn't embrace the atmosphere more, share my accomplishments with others on the day, or be a part of other people's journeys. This reluctance would continue to be something that I would struggle with, even to this day.

Gun timing is your time once the horn is blown, regardless of where you are. Chip timing is your time between the start gantry and the finish gantry. I didn't notice at the time, but there was a mat that I ran over at the start that started my chip time, and, at the end, there was another mat that stopped my time. So, the chip time is the time that should be used to compare run distances. This meant that my first official 10K run was timed at 01:10:10, officially my new 10K PB.

There were three important things that I took away from my first official race:

1. If the race entry states that no headphones allowed, I will check to see if it is just a suggestion or whether it would prompt disqualification. For this race, I later found out that it was just a suggestion. I then discovered (to my delight) that the Great North Run allowed the use of headphones – huzzah!
2. My focus bubble needs to be more transparent. Having this laser-beam perspective didn't allow me to enjoy the moment, meet new people, or really feel the race day magic.
3. Running with people was tricky. For the first few miles I was dodging and weaving like I was the car in the retro video game Spy Hunter. What was it going to be like with 57,000 runners?

What I did know was that there were many firsts for me that day. It was my first 10K race, my first run without stopping, my first race without music, and a first PB for a 10K run. What I didn't know was that this was going to be the first of 10 races I would take part in this year, including the Great North Run. This event well and truly opened the flood gates.

MILE 8

An Accidental Half Marathon

From this point on, with every run, every step, and every breath, the Great North Run was on my mind. I had no idea if I could do it and I had no confidence in my ability to run 13.1 miles. After running over 800 miles since my first run on that fateful day in 2014, I still didn't really see myself as a runner. I was just a fat bloke who ran.

It was a regular Saturday and a standard run; the weather was overcast with intermittent rain. I had just finished a mundane local 10K with gas still in the tank (so to speak). I then made the conscious decision to do an extra downhill stretch right next to my house. In my head I was thinking,

'Just this downhill run, then walk back up our local secret snicket, then home and a hot shower, done.'

My legs had other ideas; at the bottom of the hill they went left instead of right toward the snicket. It literally felt like I had twisted my body 180 degrees at the waist. My top half wanted to go one way and my bottom half wanted to go the other. My legs just took over, and before I knew it, I was at the Denby Dale train station for the second time that day. It was at this turnaround point that my legs just decided to stop working as if to say,

'Ok, that's it, we're done!'

The issue now was that I was at the furthest point away from my front door. Luckily, my head didn't hold a grudge, it just stepped up and took over as if to say,

'Let's do this!'

It was a major struggle; probably the hardest thing I had done to date running wise. I got back to the street my house was on and looked at my GPS watch, it said 12.4 miles. Two loops of my 10K or 6.2-mile route, which made sense. There were two things in that moment that I had to get my head around:

1. I was only 0.7 miles away from completing a half marathon distance; and
2. How the hell was I still upright!?

I must have done 10 to 15 lengths of my street back and forth to make the distance on my watch say 13.1. The curtain-twitching neighbours must have thought I was nuts.

I fell into the house like I did with my kidney stone pain, just over a year ago. This time I was in pain, but it was a good pain. My wife Wendy took one look at me and said, annoyed and concerned,

'Where the hell have you been? I was just about to get in the car to come and look for you.'

I guess I was so focused on the distance, I hadn't realised I was out for over four hours. All I said with a smile and a look of disbelief was,

'I just ran a half marathon – for fun!' Then it hit me, as my lips were dry as a bone, and I added,

'Without water.'

It was all recorded, so it really happened. When I posted my achievement on Facebook, my running friends were impressed but concerned about my mistake of not bringing water, which I now know is very dangerous. I think the reason I hadn't given drinking water a second thought was the fact it was raining during my run.

To say I was sore the next day was the understatement of the year. However, the overwhelming sense of accomplishment made it easier to deal with, until I had to use the stairs. As I clung to the handrail for dear life and walked up or down the stairs, it was like I had two full length casts on my legs. I thought to myself,

'What the hell …? When does this pain stop?!'

It took me about 10 days to be able to walk normally. During that time, I framed my medal and race number I received for the Wakefield 10K race, added the date and official time and hung it on the wall near my bed for inspiration. I then visualised the frame that I would create for the Great North Run, adorned with a medal and items to mark the race that took me 10 years to build enough confidence and stamina to run.

Following the Wakefield 10K success, and as part of my Great North Run prep, I entered the Manchester 10K road race that was to be held in May and the Leeds 10K in July. These two races got me thinking …

'If I know I can run the 13.1 distance, and I need more experience running with people, what's stopping me from entering some prep half marathons?'

The answer to that question was … 'Nothing!'

MILE 9

2015 The Blackpool Half Marathon

Being a Barnsley lass, and living in the Denby Dale area for most of her life, Wendy's favourite place to visit is Blackpool. When we first got married and later, as a family of four, we would go to Blackpool at least once a year. Wendy would regale me with her stories of how her family visited Blackpool many times during her childhood, which created vivid memories for her. This all came crashing down one Christmas, when the topic of Blackpool came up during a family dinner conversation; Wendy started telling us all about her precious memories of joyous family jaunts to Blackpool, and what a pleasure it was to build memories as a family playing in the sand and riding the donkeys, only to be stopped mid story by her parents, who stated that they only remember going to Blackpool once when they were young and, in fact, never really liked Blackpool at all … ouch!

I knew that when a potential visit to Blackpool was on the cards, Wendy's buy in would be instantaneous. The 2015 Blackpool Half Marathon was to be held on 26th April. As I already knew I could run the distance, all I needed to find out was what the slowest person's time was, and the number of runners in the previous year's race. In 2014, there were 983 finishers with the last runner crossing the line at 04:35:02. I was concerned about only having 983 runners and a potential cut off time, which, for this event was increased because the half marathon was on the same day as the Blackpool marathon; this added another 401 finishers. The last runner of the 2014 Marathon came in at 06:46:34, which would, essentially, be the cut off. I hoped that my time would be well inside that. Once the potential cut off time was sorted, I then researched the next most important feature of any race I now entered … yes, headphones were, in fact, allowed during this race.

The plan was that we would drive up on the day, I would run my race, spend a little family time at the Pleasure Beach, and drive home the same day. I got the thumbs up for the plan from Wendy and, with three or four clicks of the mouse, I entered my first official half marathon.

I didn't do any formal training for this race, I just increased my distance and frequency of runs. I only had four weeks to prepare but felt quietly optimistic that I could finish. During the build up to Blackpool, I didn't do another accidental half marathon. The only thing I did differently was experiment with isotonic gels to find out the best time to take them and which ones didn't upset my stomach.

I also hydrated myself quite regularly with my newly bought Nike waist hydration kit (water bottle to the rest of us). The longest run I did during those four weeks was a 10-mile run. My times didn't matter during this informal training, as I was confident I would finish within the six-hour cut off I set for myself, unless something catastrophic happened. At this point, I was mentally and physically set; this race was a means to an end as all my hopes and fears were focused on the Great North Run.

The race number was not posted out for this race; it had to be picked up at the Blackpool Hilton on the day. I knew this place well, not because I could afford to stay there, but because we saw it every time we visited. This meant we would have to be there early to register and receive the race day pack. It's an hour and 42-minute drive from our house to Blackpool and the race started at 10:00am. I went through my night-before routine of laying out my running kit, Nike shoes, Nike running tights, Nike baggy shorts (still not confident to just wear the tights), gels, headphones, hydration belt, and my Canadian cycling jersey. The three pockets came in handy for my gels and a few bananas. The obligatory picture, which essentially was my laundry, was taken and posted on all my social networking platforms. Now, off to bed for an early night. Sleep before a race? It hasn't happened yet.

I was up before the annoying morning buzzer went off and realised the pre-race pasta feast must have been digested, as my stomach was already grumbling. To solve this problem, I had two sachets of golden syrup oatmeal, three pieces of toast, two bananas, my multivitamin, and, of course, my vitamin C + zinc. The family was up, but I was changed and ready to go before anyone else. I got my race outfit on and we were out the door at 6:31am. I gave myself two hours of drive time, 30 minutes to get registered and 45 minutes to enjoy the atmosphere and enter my focus bubble. The plan looked great on paper.

About 30 minutes into the drive, my feet started throbbing, I had tied my shoes way too tight in all the excitement. I pulled over and released the building pressure and then carried on like it never happened. After 90 minutes of mundane driving, I knew we were getting close as Wendy's giddiness rose from a two to a ten. We had finally arrived in Blackpool; I suggested parking on the Pleasure Beach side in the Sandcastle Water Park car park. I would then slowly run to the Hilton as a warmup, while the family got a proper breakfast, and I would meet up with them in, approximately, four hours. Again, it looked great on paper.

This time there were a few hiccups with the plan. Firstly, with any pre-race excitement there is a need for, let's just say, a not-so-quiet visit to the loo, but the water park was not open yet, so I had to make a mad dash across the street to the Wetherspoon's pub. Secondly, once the well-wishing family hugs and kisses were given, I started my slow warmup run to the Hilton. After about 25 minutes, the Hilton was still nowhere to be seen. I thought for sure it was just over the hill, as it had seemed to be every time we visited Blackpool. I had never had to run to it from the water park before. I looked at my watch; I had run two miles and it seemed like it was going to be another few miles before I reached the hotel. So, I did what every embarrassed and already tired runner with a Canadian maple leaf on their chests did in these situations – I took the local tram the rest of the way and played the proper Canadian tourist role to a tee. Ironically, because it was actually only another 0.8 to go, I got off the tram at the next stop. All I can say is that 0.8 of a mile looks like 10 miles when you're nervous about being late for your first official half marathon.

With two miles under my belt and another 13.1 to go, I felt tired and more nervous than ever as I picked up my race number. In my race envelope, there was the number 1309, four small pins, and a strip of paper with some sort of electronic circuit on the front; the instructions on how to attach it to your shoe were on the back. I knew what a timing chip looked like as I had been the event coordinator for the Leeds Half Marathon in 2005 and 2008, but I had never seen anything like this. After I awkwardly asked the volunteer what it was, I quickly tried to blend into the crowd before I could hear the laughter due to the volunteer telling others that the fat guy didn't know what a chip timing strip was. That probably never happened, but it did in my head.

With my race number on, timing strip fastened, headphones ready, and standing next to the 4 hours+ placard, I was ready to go. It was getting busy in the starting funnel, and once again the atmosphere was electric with everybody chatting nervously to whoever was in ear shot, while a DJ played loud music. The backdrop to the race was a breath-taking view of the sea and the weather was glorious. Maybe too glorious as I adjusted my hydration belt and rechecked my water supply. I took some pictures of the crowd and posted them, probably with some clever wording, but, at the same time, I was getting mentally prepared for my first official half marathon. I was now entering my focus bubble, with a laser beam focus just on finishing the race.

The horn sounded at exactly 10:00 am and we were off. It only took me just over one minute to cross the starting mat, which I took a mental note of this time, pushing the button on my GPS watch. I double checked it to make sure it was working, cranked up the four-hour long playlist on my iPod Nano, and played dodge and weave for the first 100 metres. This was actually happening – I was running a half marathon!

I had settled into what I thought was a comfortable pace, but looked down at my watch, only to let out a loud,

'DAMN IT!' seeing that my first mile pace was 12:45.

'WAY TOO FAST!' I shouted.

I could have sworn I saw people give me that 'what a newb' look, as my disappointment was overheard by the other runners.

I had even repeated the phrase over and over again in the starting funnel,

'Don't start off too fast.'

Knowing I was probably going to pay for that later, I slowed to my usual comfortable pace of a 14-minute mile.

The route started as a loop, then went out and back along the seaside promenade. There were hills, but due to my training in hilly Denby Dale, it was nothing I couldn't handle. The start of the race went from the Hilton towards Pleasure Beach, where I left Wendy, Ross, and Tasha. It would have been great to see them, but I think they must have been still eating breakfast. As I passed our car park, I scanned the cheering crowd for their familiar faces. All I saw were other people's family's faces and well-wishing handmade signs. I hunkered down with 11.1 miles to go.

In the beginning, avoiding a heart attack, a stroke, and diabetes were the main reasons for me starting my running journey, but it was more than that when running became the fabric of who I was. As a parent, you always want to be a hero to your kids – to be somebody whom they look up to. I have always considered that my parents were heroes to me. My mum, for her independence and willingness to take risks. My dad, for his kind heart and generosity. I hoped that, someday, my kids would understand that this journey I was on, was for them. I say these words because I didn't know how much my journey was for their benefit until we locked eyes during the sixth mile. I was finishing my loop and was back in front of pleasure beach and there they were. My heart filled with delight when I saw Wendy, Ross, and Tasha cheering for me; it was as if time had stopped. The look on their faces filled my heart with what I could only describe as sheer pride. I felt, at that moment, my family were proud that I was their dad and husband. The kids ran beside me for about 200 metres and, during that space of time, my focus bubble evaporated, and I well and truly embraced this wonderous moment. That moment has stuck with me to this day.

I felt comfortable moving past the 7th mile and I was now moving along the promenade running in the opposite direction to the finish line. I kept thinking I should surely be turning back soon. It felt like I was running forever and my legs kept reminding me of this fact. My pace slowed and my legs ached. I finally made the turn and was now heading towards the finish. Making this turn gave me a bit of a boost, knowing I had only 3 miles to go. Even though I was running at the rate of a 15-minute mile, I caught up with this random guy who was the same physical size as me. He was wearing shorts over his running tights, sunglasses, an 80's style fabric headband, and big, over-the-ear Beats headphones. We never did speak, we just exchanged glances as if to say,

'What the hell are we doing here and how far away is the bloody finish?!'

In our now two-person race to the finish, the leader changed a few times. His strategy was to run for a bit, then walk for a bit. So, when he ran, he would pass me; when he walked, I would pass him. My strategy would be to stay at the consistent break-neck speed of a, now, 16-minute mile.

This race for the ages ended at the last mile when I left this kindred spirit in the dust. At mile 12, I turned on the boosters. During this final stretch, it felt like I was doing a 7-minute mile, but according to my GPS watch, it was only 14. I was on my way to finishing my first official half marathon. There are two things that I remember from this race; one is the thrilled looks on my kids' faces at mile 6, and, two was this awkwardly steep hill that was on a sharp turn at mile 13.

'Who the hell puts a hill here, at the end of a race?' I asked out loud.

This time nobody was around to hear me. At the top of this bastard hill, 200 metres away, was the finishing gantry, a glorious sight. I crossed the finish at 02:56:23. I broke three hours! WTF?

A banana, an XXL t-shirt, a goody bag, and a race medal that could only be described as a toothpick, were given to me separately, which meant, at the end of the gauntlet I had to juggle several items at once, while breathing heavily, sweating, looking for my family, and dealing with the fact that I was in absolute shock.

The race medal was very thin; its width was about the size of a watch strap. It was in the form of the famous Blackpool Tower. Due to its size, it's not one of my favourites.

The best thing a runner can get at the end of any race is a hug and a smile from family or friends; it makes all the hard work well worth it. In every race so far, my focus bubble has popped as soon as I cross the finish line and I try and embrace the accomplishment to its fullest.

The rest of the day was all about the family, hobbling, wobbling, and watching the kids dart from ride to ride in Nickelodeon Land at the Blackpool Pleasure Beach. I mostly watched from, what I felt was, the most comfortable steel benches in North West England.

MILE 10

Yet Another Newb Mistake

After my successful Wakefield 10K race and the Blackpool Half Marathon, I started entering races left, right, and centre to get some more Great North Run prep in. Local, regional, or national – I didn't care. If an event took place before the Great North Run I was entering it. I well and truly had the runner's bug.

The 2015 Manchester 10K road race on 10th May was another well-organised event by the Run For All team, with over 22,000 participants. The main story of this race was the result of my pre-race phobia of being late. I parked in the first car park I saw once I arrived in the centre of Manchester. Then, in my post-race daze, I forgot where I parked. I finished the 10K race in 01:14:35, but it took me 02:38:35 to find my car – true story. This was not good; I was shivering, tired, and almost in tears until I eventually found the hidden carpark. Manchester would become a city that would not be kind to me during my running journey.

On 12th July, three days after my 45th birthday, I ran in the 2015 Leeds 10K. This was a tough run; one type of weather that I was not used to running in, was the heat. It was hot on that day, which was reflected in my finishing time of 01:20:33.

Most of August 2015 was spent doing training runs ranging, in distance, from 3 to 11 miles. I felt confident in my ability to run with people around me, so I just needed to get the miles in and keep my fitness up until the big day.

In a race entry frenzy, I had inadvertently entered two other half marathons very close to the date of the Great North Run. It was not until I saw all three races on a calendar, that I noticed that I'd made a drastic error. The 2015 Great North Run was on 13th September, the 2015 Vale of York Half Marathon was on 20th September, and the final race I had entered in haste, was the 2015 IKANO Robin Hood Half Marathon, which took place on 27th September. This meant that I'd entered three half marathons on three consecutive weekends! What a newb. I was confident in finishing the Great North Run, but could I run three in the same number of weeks? I remembered it took me 10 days to recover from my accidental half and the Blackpool half. Was it doable, or even possible for me to accomplish such a herculean task? Well, we were going to find out, as I posted my new personal three half marathons in three weeks challenge on Facebook. To quote Pharaoh Rameses II, 'so it shall be written, so it shall be done'.

MILE 11

Prep Time Was Over

On 13th September 2015, there were more than 57,000 runners taking part in the 35th Great North Run, starting in Newcastle-upon-Tyne and finishing in Gateshead. Just with the sheer size of the event, I knew there would be many sights and stories to behold. Before the day, when I told people I was running in the event, they always started their stories with these four words:

'Oooh, you'll love it'!

They then continued telling me their favourite memories. I would listen to every word with wide-eyed enthusiasm as I wanted practical tips that would help me with my run, and I wanted to hear about iconic events during the race to ensure I did not miss them.

'The British Red Arrows fly over as you finish', a veteran runner of the event told me. This must have been very emotional at the time because the memory alone brought them to tears.

'During the last mile, the road is five people deep and they're yelling your name, because your first name is on your race number', shared another enthusiastic runner.

I heard stories of the unwavering support en route, with kids setting up tables with orange slices and gummy bears, handing them to the runners as they passed.

There was also a tradition of yelling at the top of your lungs 'Oggy Oggy Oggy' followed by a reply of 'Oi Oi Oi' from other runners, under the first over pass. In my mind, it was going to be the run that topped all runs.

With a hotel room booked, my race number 52274 at hand, all the research done, and my race day bag checked and double checked, I was now ready for the 114-mile journey to Newcastle, which, according to my sat nav, was 2 hours and 2 minutes away.

All that was left was an emotional send off from my family. All the hugs, kisses, chest bumps, high fives, tears, laughter, and well wishes were all locked in my heart, ready to use during the race. Just as I was about to get in the car, I returned to the door, popped my head back into the house and yelled,

'Hey luv, I'm going to run the Great North Run this weekend!'

MILE 12

The 2015 Great North Run

Note to self: as part of your race prep, check the weather forecast. It was chucking it down when I arrived at the Premier Inn my wife had booked just outside Newcastle. It was Saturday 12th September and the plan was to check in, get some food, then go to the race village and soak up the pre-race atmosphere. Plus, there was a bonus; as part of the weekend, there was an international athletics competition right in the heart of the city.

Catching a glimpse of the games on BBC One, it was quite a marvel to behold. There were different athletic events being held on makeshift platforms, which were set on main roads between large office buildings in the centre of Newcastle. It would have been great to see it in person, but the rain was relentless and came down in large drops, which formed major puddles. It didn't seem to affect these world-class athletes sprinting and jumping: talk about focus! After talking to the reception staff at the hotel, a taxi would have been expensive as the hotel I was staying in was off the beaten track. I did think about driving in, but when it's raining hard and you don't know where you're going, that's just a disaster waiting to happen. Looking back, these were probably all 'focus bubble' excuses, which, once again, stopped me from embracing the moment.

So, there I sat, alone with my thoughts in my hotel room. Well that was a lie – I was with another person who was lying on my bed. Another lie – it was only the outline of a person on my bed. I had laid out my running gear in the shape of a person. My headband, headphones, Canadian cycling jersey, my race number, gels, my long-sleeved Nike compression shirt, hydration belt, Nike running pants, baggy Nike running shorts (still not confident enough to ditch the shorts), Nike socks and my Glycerine 13 Brooks running shoes. I called this flat man 'Miles'. I'm not going to lie and say I didn't have an extensive conversation with Miles in my room, because I did. Miles was a great listener.

I don't have a picture of 'Miles' the day I named him. However, this is a picture of the day he was born. This is the picture of the first time I took a picture of what was, essentially, my laundry and my race number. Laying out my running gear and snapping a picture started with my first official race – the 2015 Wakefield 10K. It then became a pre-race tradition.

The next day, on no sleep, I was up early. I set out two pots of instant oatmeal, two bananas, and a bottle of water on the hotel desk; it looked like they were fronted on the edge of an ASDA shelf. These items were soon to be in my stomach giving me the fuel to finish this race, or at least start it. I slowly dismantled Miles and within 45 minutes I was dressed, fed, and ready to go. After one more chat with reception staff to ask the best way to the race finish car park in Gateshead, I was soon in my car and on the way to run a race in which I had only dreamed of participating in 2004. I had to park at the finish as the race was one-way, Newcastle to Gateshead. We (the runners) then had to board a bus to the start line in Newcastle. On arriving at the car park I was pleased with myself; another perk of being an early bird is that you usually get your choice of parking spots.

There were people milling around but it was not overly busy. I had set a pre-arranged time and place to meet some friends who were veteran Great North Runners. Tracy Hughes, David Lee, and Gav Beardshall were all running in the event. They'd all brought supporters to cheer them on. The group soon took me under their respective wings as they must have seen my overwhelmed expression. They dragged me onto the bus, they dragged me off the bus, they dragged me to the least-used porta loo (veterans know all the tricks of the trade), and after some good luck hugs and words of encouragement, the group divided so we could all go to our pre-designated starting areas.

As predicted, my starting area or 'pen', was at the back of the pack. The starting pen positions were allocated when you filled in your entry form. A four-hour predicted finishing time meant I started at the furthest point away from the finish line, which was fine; I was comfortable in that position. The area that I was standing in, had now got busy with nervous runners trying to find their way to their respective starting positions. For me, the issue was that the distance between my current position, and where I needed to be, seemed further than some of the prep races I had run.

To help me and ensure I didn't wig out before the race started, one of my running heroes David Lee was standing right beside me with his arm around my shoulders. David had run four marathons, an Ironman Triathlon, and had run the Great North Run 11 times. He was working toward his running coaching certification and was going to run with some of the runners he had been training. He had taken a group of five non-runners from just walking, to running, to running a half marathon. David has always been a true inspiration and having him with me was a Godsend. I had no idea where I needed to be, so I stuck to David like a scared kid sticks to his parents in a busy shopping centre.

The area was now heaving with people; it was awe-inspiring and terrifying at the same time. We walked along the gated fence as people entered their starting areas, which had coloured signs corresponding with the colours on their race bibs. I passed yellow, green, purple, blue, red, orange, and pretty much every colour in the rainbow except mine, pink. It seemed like we were walking for ages until we reached the back of the pack.

I had finally made it to the start of the Great North Run; a part of me was in disbelief. The number of people was intimidating at first, but as I looked round, I saw people stretching, jumping up and down, chatting with fellow runners, and much to my relief I saw people who were just as petrified as I was. They all had their own stories to tell, their own journey to how they reached this moment. Even though I felt insignificant standing in this sea of people, I felt part of something bigger. I took a moment to think that maybe – just maybe – as the 2015 Great North Run was about to start, there was an overweight person, eating crisps and drinking a Coke, flipping channels with their own journey to start. Just like I had, just a year ago.

Before I knew it, the time had come; the horn was blown, and the race started. It was time to finish my Great North Run story that was now 11 years in the making; it was time to conquer my emotions and run this race; it was time to show my kids that anything was possible if you set your mind to it. Actually, it was, once again, time to hurry up and wait. The elite runners started first, then the club runners, then yellow, green, purple, blue, red, orange … you get the point. Let's just say it took the people wearing the pink bibs so long just to get to the start line that Mo Farah of Great Britain and Mary Keitany of Kenya had both finished their run before we'd even set off! Mo finished in 59:22 and Mary finished in 01:07:32. They both ran 13.1 miles faster than I ran 6.2 miles (10K). Unbelievable!

After 74 minutes of slow walking, I eventually crossed the start line, I started my watch, pounded my chest with my fist twice and pointed to the sky thinking, 'I am here, doing this for me, and everyone who supported me. Let's do this!' I then entered an extreme version of my focus bubble, laser focused on getting it done. So much so, I could barely hear the bass thumping club mix I had blasting through my headphones. I consciously started off slowly and took one mile at a time. I approached the first underpass and thought this must be the 'Oggy Oggy Oggy' tunnel, and just like clockwork, before I could finish my thought,

'Oggy Oggy Oggy!' was yelled followed by another person yelling,

'Oi Oi Oi!', followed by a few laughs and cheers.

First tradition at the Great North Run experienced – tick.

My fastest pace reached the pace of 12-minute miles, but then I seemed to systematically slow down. Tired legs or mental exhaustion from being in such an intense focus bubble? Both? I couldn't pinpoint the reason, but I was definitely getting slower. My speed reduced to 14-, 15-, then 16-minute miles; what was going on? All of this struck me at the 8th mile; I thought I was running at a fast pace, swinging my arms hard, and breathing heavily. I then looked around at other runners and they were bloody walking … AND GAINING ON ME! I must have looked like a right idiot, because I felt like one. Was it the dreaded runners wall? Had my body just given up on the 11-year mission? Or was my mind just telling me,

'You're not a runner and you don't really deserve to be here'?

I don't know what it was at the time, but my Great North Run experience just seemed to get worse.

I got to the point of the race at which people were finished with cheering and were retreating back into their houses. The promise of tables filled with orange slices and gummy bears distributed by enthusiastic kids was replaced by barren tables with the odd orange rind, and empty Haribo plastic wrappers being blown down the street and sidewalk. From a distance I could hear the roar of the crowd at the finish, they cheered the British Red Arrows as they flew over the finishing area. From where I was, I could only see the trail of white jet stream smoke. Missing these iconic Great North Run moments only made me go slower. I was fed up, my legs started to ache like never before. I then remembered something and mumbled to myself,

'Shit … I have to do this again in seven days! What the hell was I thinking?'

It was the last mile, and there were no cheering crowds five people deep, only the occasional,

'Go on, Canada!', as I was wearing my Canadian cycle jersey.

I think I heard two people shout, 'Well done, Sean!' (my name was on my number).

With my legs aching, shoulders drooping, and feet dragging, I could finally see the finish of this 11-year dream and it was glorious. With 100 metres left, the hours of training, all the hopes and fears, and the support of friends and family hit me like a tsunami, and the waves of emotion came flowing out in the form of tears. A feeling of disbelief, exhaustion, exhilaration and just an overwhelming sense of accomplishment took over, and I started to hyperventilate while trying to hold back the tears in front of the volunteers as I crossed the finish line. I soon realised that I could not conceal this much emotion as a finishing funnel volunteer saw that I was in a bit of distress and struggling to breathe and asked if I was ok. I took a minute, caught my breath and emotions, and said yes. Even though I was caught in the moment, I did remember to get my phone out to video my emotions for a special episode of 'Sean Speaks' Episode #160: Three Half Marathons for the charity ME Challenge, which can be seen on YouTube.

I had done it, but if I'm honest, as I walked back to the car alone, in pain and emotionally drained, it felt like a hollow accomplishment. Was it due to not having any friends or family at the end to embrace and enjoy the moment with? Had it not really hit me yet? Did I overhype the experience in my head, like I often do with going to new movies in a theatre, later to be disappointed as the movie did not achieve my high expectations that I had in my head? Or was it the fact the accomplishment of running the Great North Run was only part of a bigger challenge: three half marathons in three weekends? To this day I am unable to answer that. All I do know is that when I watch the Great North Run on BBC One now, I can say, 'Been there done that, got the XL t-shirt that was too damn small.'

My final thought about the Great North Run is that my experience was not the best. I am glad I did it but will not be doing it again. I feel it is for the fast runners who are able to experience the time-sensitive iconic events surrounding the day. Maybe I am just bitter about the fact I can't run fast; I'm not built for speed and I ran my one and only Great North Run in 03:39:48. At the end of the day, it was never about the time, it was about fulfilling a goal that I set for myself and the opportunity to test my limits. With this being said, my limits still had not been tested; I had two more half marathons to run in the next 14 days and I wondered whether that would break me.

Overwhelmed with emotion and my accomplishment, I crossed the finish line at the 2015 Great North Run. I honestly could not believe I did it. At that moment, I remembered lying on the futon, drinking Coke, and eating crisps 11 years earlier. My emotions in this picture reflect how far I had come.

MILE 13

Ice Bath

Sitting in a car for a few hours after running 13.1 miles was probably not the best thing for my legs. As I arrived home and put the car into park, I pondered how I was going to hoist myself out, up the three stairs to the front door, and then up the 18 stairs to take a hot shower. It didn't take as long as running a half marathon, but it did take me the same amount of time as running a leisurely 5K.

After a glorious hot shower and still feeling conflicted about my accomplishment, my focus needed to turn to the next half marathon that was happening in only seven days. However, at this point, I felt that there was ABSOLUTELY no way I would be able to run another half marathon in that short space of time; my legs were just way too sore. The silver lining to this story, was that the next two races were local, so no hotels were needed, and relative to the Great North Run entry fee, the fee for the next two races were mere pittance. What this meant to me was, if I decided to pass on the next race I would not be that much out of pocket. Plus, I was pretty sure I would be ready for the race in 14 days so I didn't lose my entry fee money for both races. It wasn't until my son, Ross, came up to me and asked,

'How are you going to run your next race, if you are so sore dad?'

I replied, 'Oh, I'll be ready, Ross,' followed by a large audible gulp.

How could I pass on my next race now?

I turned to the internet to get some focus back. The quickest way to recover from running a half marathon, was typed into the Google search bar. I didn't like what I saw, so I turned to my running network and friends on Facebook.

'I just ran the Great North Run but have another half marathon in 7 days. What's the best way to get my sore legs back to normal.'

CRAP, the replies were the same as Google's: an ice bath and foam roller. I knew that professional athletes would sit in an ice bath after a big game, so I thought if it worked for them, it would work for me. Up the stairs I went again, slowly, to run a cold bath with the half a bag of ice that looked like it had been in the freezer for years. When the tub was deep enough to cover my legs, I disrobed and reluctantly stepped in with both feet. It was cold, but I was tough, and I said to myself,

'This needs to be done.'

I squatted down to sit and submerge my legs in the cold water, which according to Google would then cause my blood vessels to tighten and drain the blood and any lactic acid out, thus enabling me to be ready for my next race. But, as my ass cheeks touched the water, I squealed

'NOPE!'

I sprung out of the bath, drained it, and had the hottest most relaxing bath, while thanking my friends for their congratulatory comments on Facebook. It was glorious.

Years later, I was told to wear shorts when you have an ice bath, use just enough water to cover your legs and if you could make it past the first two minutes of shock, you would be fine for the rest of the 10 minutes you should be in the tub. I would like to describe my next ice bath experience, but I can't, because there was never a next time much to my sports massage guy, John Hackleton's, disappointment.

The next day, I repeated the hot bath routine, still thinking there was no way I would be able to run on Sunday. Tuesday same, Wednesday same and, at this point, I was getting worried. Then I remembered, after the Blackpool Half Marathon it took me until Thursday before I could get any sort of movement back into my legs enabling me to run even a short distance. Like clockwork, on the Thursday, I went for a one-mile run; my legs were sore but they felt ok. My mind, body, and spirit were now committed to running the second of the three half marathons I had entered, but was it going to be a better experience than the Great North Run?

MILE 14

2015 Vale of York Half Marathon

Sunday 20th September 2015 was a day like any other Sunday, with clear skies and a bit of a chill in the air. However, in terms of my running journey, I was, unbelievably, about to run my second half marathon in eight days.

It was now usual for me to arrive early, but this time I may have overdone it. I arrived so early I thought I had arrived before any race volunteers. It turned out, I actually got there before the parking volunteer, and, as a consequence, I started off the direction people could park, as there were no lines. My parked car dictated the way people would park for the whole day … with great power comes great responsibility.

Registration had a line of one – me. I got my race number (813), the timing chip for my shoe, then played the early bird waiting game, which consisted of sitting cross legged on a concrete slab to wait for 35 minutes until the second person registered. The Vale of York Half Marathon was a small race with just over 1,200 runners. It was held at a small airport with the start of the race on a runway, which was kind of cool. As I waited and looked at the one- and two-seater light aircrafts that were being worked on by some mechanics who had no interest in what was going on around them, I saw people who looked familiar from other local races I had run. Did this mean I'd become a regular? Prior to me entering my focus bubble, a few people from parkrun came over to wish me luck and we chatted about past and future races, which was nice. For me, this race would become typical for an event of this size. Start at the back, struggle between the 9th and 12th mile, and finish strong but last – standard. I finished The Vale of York Half Marathon in 03:07:36 and was the last male runner.

The post-race routine was, get medal, get the 'never fit' t-shirt, and return to the car. However, this time it felt different; it almost felt I had become complacent with these races; I felt a sense of accomplishment and the runner's high was still there, but it was missing something. Had I lost my enthusiasm for the challenge or for running? It may have been down to the fact that I was sore, wanted a hot bath, or the idea that doing it again in seven days was nonsense. THAT thought was instantly blocked from my mind. However, during my drive home, I did ask myself whether I had set the bar too high with this silly challenge? With one more to go, I was going to have to dig deep to achieve it.

MILE 15

My Body is A-Changing

The first 'later-in-life' body changes started within days of turning 40. In 2010, I was definitely not a runner and it would be four years before my kidney stone would rear its ugly head. That year, my birthday was on Friday and by the following Wednesday my body started to show 40 years of wear and tear. Just like that, my eyesight became blurry when reading. Reading labels on Pot Noodles, on my Coke, or having to read a take-away menu to pick what scrumptious meal I was going to have for our Friday night treat (all the important things) were getting tougher. It took me back a little, as it happened so suddenly.

With a quick visit to Specsavers, it was revealed I needed reading glasses with a strength of +1.50. This was the first sign that my body was changing as I slid into middle age. Over the following years, my body would continue to change, much like puberty, hair started to grow in weird places again, it was harder to lose weight, and I saw the first signs of grey hair.

Five years later, changes due to age, lifestyle, and diet were common, but things were about to get worse. Following the Vale of York Half Marathon, I avoided the ice bath squeal and went straight for my steaming hot bath recovery routine. After only two days, like magic, my legs recovered faster than the previous week. I did a light run on the Wednesday and felt fully recovered by the Friday – brilliant! This was amazing, as I was now ready to finish this challenge. I was excited about my next race: the 2015 IKANO Robin Hood Half Marathon. I was so enthusiastic and confident that I upgraded my entry to a VIP status, which included access to the VIP Finish Line Tent, a free post-race photograph, and the main reason for the upgrade, a post-race massage, I thought I deserved it.

The exhilaration turned to anxiousness after what I discovered after a light recovery run four days before my third half marathon in three weeks – a bump in a weird place.

MILE 16

I Blame the iPhone Not my Age or Obesity

I was reluctant to include this bit in this book as it is embarrassing, a bit cringeworthy, and probably something people don't want to hear about. However, as it was the third race of a three-race challenge, I figured that leaving out details of this race and the 'other thing' I was struggling with, would make it conspicuous in its absence. I then thought, I may not be the only person who had experienced what happened to me, and hope others can find it in their heart to understand and empathise with people who have endured this type of pain or embarrassment. You have been warned.

In the shower, after a light three-mile run four days before the next race, I felt something; a weird bump on my ass. Following my shower, with some clever angles and gymnastics, I was able to get a picture of this bump on my ass using an iPad. What I saw was a large Costco sized plum between my ass cheeks. What it turned out to be, after a quick visit to Dr Google was an external haemorrhoid. Reading on, I found that haemorrhoids were caused by things such as obesity and sitting for long periods of time on the toilet. What I also found out was, after you turn 40, your body is more susceptible to things like this. This new information now put my next challenge in jeopardy.

It didn't hurt; it just felt really uncomfortable and seemed to be getting bigger. With an emergency visit to my local doctor on the Thursday and after an embarrassing visual inspection, it was explained to me that haemorrhoids develop when the veins of the rectum or anus become dilated or enlarged and can be internal or external. External haemorrhoids are usually found beneath the skin surrounding the anus. Mine was external and the plum colour was because it was basically a large pouch filled with blood. Getting rid of it would require me to have an operation that would probably be in a few weeks' time, and there were no quick options to get this thing off my ass.

I knew it was bad when the doctor asked me to 'spread 'em' and the first words out of her mouth was,

"WOW! THAT'S BIG!'

After an awkward silence, I asked the doctor if she thought I could still run a half marathon. She responded in a tone that kind of questioned why anyone would want to run a half marathon with that bulbous mass on their ass. She said,

'Uuuumm, there is a risk of it popping as the pouch will rub. This could lead to infection if not treated. Plus, it will make quite a mess because it's a giant bag of blood!'

Infection and big mess, were not good words, but I noticed that she didn't say no. So, the question was, should I risk it? It felt uncomfortable when I walked, but, ironically, not when I ran. I took this as this as a sign and decided I was willing to risk it.

Once I made the decision, my pre-race prep routine began. Miles was lying on the floor at the base of my bed, the porridge oats and bananas were ready for eating in the kitchen, and an alarm was set for an early wake up. This was exactly what I had done the previous two Saturday nights. The only difference was that, on this night, I tried to put out of my mind the fact that there was a ticking time bomb on my ass that could explode at any second.

As a side note, let's just say from now on, I do all my Facebook updates and posts, or use my iPhone to search, read memes, and watch video clips, while sitting on the couch and not on the toilet.

MILE 17

2015 IKANO Robin Hood Half Marathon

This half marathon had over 6,000 entrants, plus with over 1,000 people running the full marathon, it was a big field of runners of all shapes and sizes. Just like the proverbial issues faced by Goldilocks in the fairy-tale, The Great North Run was too big, The Vale of York Half was too small, but this event was just right!

Once again, the early bird didn't catch the worm as I arrived too early at the VIP tent to find people scrambling to set up. In the tent, there were long folding tables, wooden benches, and tables for the post-race massages that I was so looking forward to. I hung around the VIP tent for a while, but I couldn't really sit down due to, well … you know what. So, before anything was set up, I left the VIP area to find the start line, get the lay of the land, and enter my focus bubble.

My haemorrhoid, which I now called Hemmie, was still there, but luckily had not increased in size. It literally felt like I had a large tennis ball between my ass cheeks, and trying to keep it there was some sort of added challenge or side bet. I strategically wore all black from the waist down just in case Hemmie's time was up. Even with this forethought I really didn't know what I would do if Hemmie popped. How would I explain a blood trail following me as I ran, without people gipping or being disgusted? At this point, my mindset was prepared for the worst and I hoped for the best. The only person who knew about my situation was Wendy and the texts came in thick and fast, asking how I was, and how 'it' was. I never told anyone about the ticking time bomb strapped to my ass during this race, and I never thought I would ever share this experience with anyone in a book. If I can raise awareness of runners with Hemmies, and help one-person deal with the stigma, I have done my job with this chapter.

The race itself was brilliant, but I was slow. Was it because it was my third half marathon in three weekends? Was it due to Hemmie? Was it my legs sticking two fingers up at me and calling me a 'knob head' for doing this ridiculous challenge? Or had I reached my running limit? I was unsure, but even though I was one of the slowest, this finish had an atmosphere I wasn't used to. The last mile was filled with supporters and well-wishers yelling, screaming, calling out my name, shouting my number 7295, and calling me Spiderman. I wasn't wearing my Canadian cycling jersey – I swapped my usual jersey for a Spiderman cycling jersey I found online. I made the change not only due to the fact I am a huge Marvel fan but because of the blue and dark red colour (not white). I then realised why there was so many cheerers at the finish. It was due to the fact that the club runners were just finishing their marathons!

I finished the race in 03:20:19, faster than the Great North Run but slower than the Vale of York Half. Yes, Hemmie was intact, but as I stopped running, I could really feel the rubbing and I was starting to get worried. I arrived at the VIP tent, posed for my complimentary post-race photo, and signed up for my post-race massage. Being one of the last in the VIP tent, the massage lines were long, and I was told it could be over a 60-minute wait. I was determined to get this massage, so I tried to sit and wait but Hemmie said NOPE, and I returned to standing. As I stood, I saw the line go down, but I also saw how hard the masseuses were working. This struck me hard in my post-race emotional state and I thought that they'd probably worked hard enough without them massaging my sweaty legs. Plus, can you imagine if Hemmie burst? I subsequently removed my name off the list and slowly limped back to my car, wearing the best medal to date, holding my goody bag, and my 'never fit' t-shirt.

So, what happened to Hemmie you might be asking? Between reflecting on my accomplishment and replying to Facebook well-wishers in a very hot steam bath, let's just say Hemmie drained peacefully and quietly away. No major clean up or explanation needed, and that's all I'm going to say about that.

MILE 18

The Day the 'M' Word was Added to my Running Vocabulary

It was now early October 2015 and, officially, I had five half marathons, three 10K road races, and one 5K mud run under my belt. I continued with half marathons and 10K races to fill my time for the rest of 2015, breaking the three-hour barrier for the second time during the 2015 Worksop Halloween Half Marathon with a time of 02:54:45. Now with 2015 coming to a close, a few runs under my belt, and many miles under my shoes, what was going to be my next challenge?

In the past, the London Marathon was something that I watched on TV each year. I used the word marathon but the 'M' word was never in my vocabulary when it came to my running journey. I applied for the London Marathon via the public lottery as a joke. I relished getting my London Marathon rejection magazine because it always includes a logoed London Marathon fleece or jacket, which was sent only if you donated your entry fee to charity. Even though it was always too small, I would squeeze into it at least once and go for a run, hoping people would see me and think I was a marathon runner. In reality, nobody noticed. However, due to the different styles and colours each year, the only thing I was promoting to the people who knew what the fleece meant, was that I got rejected for that year's London Marathon.

I vividly remember a conversation that took place during the last week of October while working with Leeds City Council. It was during this tête-à-tête with my good friend and co-council worker, John May that the 'M' word was added to my running vocabulary. I was telling John my running journey to date and he seemed generally interested when he said,

'The next thing you're going to tell me is that you're running a marathon!'

I laughed and replied, 'There is ABSOLUTELY NO WAY I will ever run a marathon, because...'

John quickly interrupted me, and said, 'I bet you will run a marathon ...'

Then John used my own words against me, '... You just told me that in 2014 you said there was ABSOLUTELY NO WAY you would ever run a half marathon! How many have you run now?'

Those words struck me because they were true. Only a few years ago, I would have never contemplated running a 10K let alone a half marathon. Hell, I had just done three half marathons over three consecutive weekends. Plus, it was really weird for me to say this out loud, but I felt I could now run a half marathon without much training. Had I turned a corner? Was the reason I was losing passion for running down to the fact that I didn't have a running challenge looming? Was a marathon something I needed to do, to take my running to the next level? Was this what was missing? Was I ready? Could I do it?

Before we move on and answer those questions, let's just take a step back and put this 'marathon absurdity' into perspective. If I were to say to you, that in two years' time, Steven Spielberg would buy the rights to this book, direct a movie based on it, and win an academy award for best picture, what would you think? Your current reaction would be comparable to mine right now with the thought of running a marathon in 2016. BEYOND IMPOSSIBLE!

However, once this marathon seed had been planted in my brain, it was hard to get rid of. So, from this point on, everything became surreal. Searching for a local marathon on Google felt weird. Thinking of producing a training plan for running a marathon felt strange. Just considering running a marathon felt downright dreamlike. As my latest 'joke' entry to the London Marathon had just been rejected, any marathon I picked was going to have to be a big one, ensuring a big field of runners. In 2016, the two events in contention were the Yorkshire Marathon on 9th October and the Greater Manchester Marathon on 10th April.

What tipped the balance was that the Yorkshire Marathon only had just over 3,500 runners in 2015, and The Greater Manchester Marathon had over 9,500 in the same year. Easing into 2016, I felt I was in the best shape of my life and I didn't want to wait until October, so I focused more on the Greater Manchester Marathon. I would never had guessed that 2016 would be filled with some unbelievable achievements and major heartbreaks.

MILE 19

Marathon Prep: The Floodgates Open

It took some courage and time to get my head around what I was about to do, but on 2nd December 2015, I decided to commit. With a few clicks of the mouse and after filling in a few web-based fields, I had officially entered a marathon. It was one year, nine months, and four days since I crossed the threshhold of my front door to start Day One, Week One of the C25K app in February 2014. What the hell was I thinking? But, I can tell you one thing for sure – my enthusiasm for running returned almost instantly.

After receiving my confirmation email, my head was spinning, buzzing, and felt like it was about to explode. I only had 130 days before I was at the start line of my first marathon. What the hell do I do now? How do I train? How many miles do I need to do? How am I going to track my progress? What do I eat? How am I going to deal with the laughter when I tell people I'm training for a marathon? It took time for this colossal challenge to feel real, but, after a few days, I became focused using a simple technique: visualisation. For everything that I did from that point forward, I only had one singular focus. I decided to have only one image in my mind, every day, all day: the finishing gantry at the 2016 ASICS Greater Manchester Marathon.

My first stop was Google to find 'The Best Marathon Training books'. There were many, but after reading the reviews I added a few to my basket and knew they would be in my hand's tomorrow, thanks to Amazon Prime. To start with, I bought 'Marathon: the ultimate running guide' by Hal Higdon, 'Marathon Training for Dummies' by Ter Stouffer Drenth, and 'The Champion's Mind' by Jim Afremow for some mental prep. As you might have guessed, two weeks of training was spent getting my head around training for a Marathon. I reread all my Men's Running magazine articles about marathons, and I talked to my running friends who had run a marathon for any advice or stories.

Two of my running mates, David Lee and Christopher Walker, both shared a short story with me from their own marathon experiences: one inspired me and one terrified me.

Christopher Walker told me the story of the time he ran his first marathon in Edinburgh, in 2009.

'It was about 28 degrees and water had been stolen from two of the water stations so was in limited supply. Police were riding up and down distributing water, and locals had hosepipes out, but it was still really hot. I hit the wall at around 22 miles and sat down, a spectator who was a runner came up to me and said, 'If you sit down now, you'll never get up – come with me'. She guided me to the next water/energy drink stop around 500 metres down the road. She made sure I got water and gels and then sent me on my way. I managed to finish in 5:38:47. I don't know who she was, but her words of encouragement and diligence in making sure I was refreshed, got me to the end.'

David Lee shared his story about the time he was running in the 2015 London Marathon. It was, again, about the dreaded wall.

'While running past the 21st and 22nd mile markers, all of a sudden people were collapsing around me. It felt like there was a sniper taking shots at runners. As they got hit, they would collapse and hit the pavement

hard. I was petrified that I, too, would be hit by the dreaded sniper and collapse.'

David never did hit the wall. He finished with a time of 04:06:54.

From left to right: Christopher Walker, Sean Kachmarski, David Lee. This selfie was taken at my 50th parkrun, at which I tried for a new personal best (PB). Even having two of my personal running heroes pacing me, it was not meant to be. My time on that day was 00:33:17, not even close. My Locke Park parkrun PB remains at 00:31:23.

In the majority of the stories I read or heard about marathon running, the wall was prevalent in most of them. It was something that was fast moving to the top of my list of things to worry about on the day. With this being said, the image of the finishing gantry would trump any negative thoughts or feelings. However, after hearing more and more stories about the wall, I started to doubt that just visualising a piece of metal scaffolding that held a clock and a finish sigh, was going to be enough to finish.

MILE 20

The Marathon Training Plan and Prep Races

After an intensive two weeks of reading books and listening to advice, it was now time to create a 16-week training schedule and log. I really had to thread the needle here as I attempted to find the balance between family, work, and training. There are apps for creating plans, but I wanted a hard copy to put on the fridge. This way, I could cross off, tick, and add the miles to a chart, creating a work of art with numbers, including a huge red circle around the big day.

I tried to keep my training plan simple by combining and modifying a few training plan examples that I had come across during my research. An Excel spread sheet would do the trick. My A3 sheet had 16 rows representing weeks down the left-hand side and along the top there were columns labelled with the days of the week, creating a grid. There were four types of runs logged on this chart; standard runs, races, long runs, and no runs. Each week, the number of miles would increase with the most miles being just before the taper. Tapering refers to the practice of reducing exercise in the days before an important competition; in my case it was two weeks before 10th April.

'Standard runs' were the runs that I would do after work or in the morning, between 1 and 6 miles in distance.

'Races' were runs that I entered and received an official race number for. I had entered a few races even before my marathon decision was made.

- 2016 Leeds Abbey Dash 10K, 6th November
- 2016 Silverstone Half Marathon, 13th March

'Long runs' were runs that I did mainly at weekends and these would be between 6 and 20 miles. What I had read (and been told) was not to run the entire distance of a marathon, which is 26.2 miles. I was told the max you should run during training should be between 21 and 23 miles, and this distance should only be done once, just before the taper. However, for my peace of mind, I decided that I would really like to run the entire distance just so I knew I could. This would mean that I would have to run a marathon for fun, which was bonkers.

'No runs' were basically rest or recovery days.

The first week of Marathon training began on Monday 21st December 2015. It was only a 12-mile week so scheduling it around Christmas was an easy thing to do, especially since I was off work due to the holidays. The first few weeks were basically the same number of miles I would do normally. However, the image of the finishing gantry in my minds-eye, motivated me to increase my pace during some runs and inspired me to add an extra hill repetition while I was out and about.

It was also at around this time that my family in Canada took notice that this running thing was not just a flash in the pan. My mum booked a trip to the UK that would coincide with me running and finishing my first marathon. This was special. To have my mum at the finish line, representing my side of the family meant a lot. The finish of this marathon journey was going to be epic.

MILE 21

Blood, Sweat, Tears, Rain, Snow, and Hail

With every run, walk, or slog, I always remained laser focused on that one image, the finishing gantry of the marathon race. With every step, I felt closer to my goal. I made a conscious decision that 80 percent of my training runs should end on an uphill near my house, to try and replicate how difficult the finish would feel at the end of the race.

Many runs tested my resolve, but there was one training run that took me to the brink. The run started wet, but by this time, running in the rain was common as I lived in England and it was winter. The temperature dropped, and the night air turned cold, cold enough to turn the rain into sleet mid run. The wind then picked up, and I was getting pelted by small sharp ice pellets, making visibility close to zero. I could barely see the brake lights of the cars that passed me. The strong wind moved the hail vertically straight into my eyes. Six miles from my house with no shelter in sight, there was only one image that kept me going, the finishing gantry, so I soldiered on. It wasn't until the fifth time a car drove past me, engulfing me with a wave one would only see on ESPN or on the Euro World Sports surfing world championships, that I thought to myself, what the hell am I doing? For a fleeting first time, I asked myself,

'Will this be worth it?'

I quickly answered that internal questions with a resounding, 'YES!' Well … if I'm honest, it was more of a sheepish, 'I bloody well hope so.'

One thing I have noticed since I started this journey is that running has enabled me to become fully in tune with my body in terms of aches, pains, energy levels, and impending sickness or injury prevention. It only happened two or three times, but at the very start of some marathon training runs, after about 100 metres my body would shout NOPE! When this happened, I would abandoned the run before it started. This may not be common practice, but all I can say is that it's been helpful for my body's well-being. To this day, no serious running injuries have stopped me running for more than a week. Also, even though I don't have any personal baseline data to prove this, the number of colds and bouts of flu that I had in the past has significantly been reduced.

The training was going well, my body was being stretched to the limit but coping, and my training races went better than expected. For the 2016 Leeds Abbey Dash 10K, I beat my 10K personal best by 8 seconds with a finishing time of 01:09:52. Even more surprising was my finishing time at the 2016 Silverstone Half Marathon.

MILE 22

2016 Silverstone Half Marathon

Only 28 days before I would be at the start of my first marathon, on 13th March, I ran my last official prep race, the Silverstone Half Marathon. This race takes place annually on the world-famous Silverstone motor racing circuit in Towcester, Northamptonshire, UK. This meant no traffic and an unusual starting time of 12:30pm. At this point in my training, I was confident about finishing and was feeling well-supported. Wendy and my two kids, Ross and Tasha, had joined me for this race on this iconic track.

It was a bitterly cold start to the day, but with just less than 10,000 runners, it soon warmed up – well, for the runners at least. This event was great for the runners, but the spectators struggled to keep warm and found it difficult to see any of the action as most were confined to the inner pit area with a limited view of the race and its runners. Now I am sure that some veterans of this race would know when and where to be to enable them to get the most out of the day. However, as a Silverstone virgin, I felt bad for my family as the atmosphere and visibility of the race was not the same as other events I had run in. Needless to say, it took some convincing for my family to join me at future non-marathon races, especially the kids. Note to self: find out if free WIFI is available for next time.

With my number securely attached, my headphones on, my new ironic DC superhero Flash cycling jersey on, and my hydration belt filled with water and gels, I was in the pen awaiting the starters' horn. There was sufficient space for me to not be in the usual sardine can situation. I found a spot in the pen that was open and comfortable. I took one last look around and I realised I was not with the three-hour pace runners; I was in front of the 02:30 pace runner. When I saw this, I just chuckled to myself and entered my focus bubble.

I am not superstitious, but on reflection it occurred to me that, almost involuntarily, I do the same three things when I step over the starting mat, and this race was no different. I ensured my Garmin was on and recording; I respectfully tapped my chest with the top of my closed fist and pointed to the sky to pay respect to my family and supporters; and started off way too fast … again!

The surface of this track was the absolute best surface to run on. No potholes, no surface cracks, no uneven surfaces, pebbles or stones. It was 13.1 miles of slick asphalt, just awesome. I had to resist making race car sounds as I ran the bends of the Formula One racetrack.

I am not sure if it was the training, the surface, my mind set, or a combination of all three, but I felt like I was motoring (no pun intended). I looked down at my watch and I had reached the pace of 10-minute miles without the accompanying heavy breathing or collapses. What the hell was going on? Had my pre-run supplement Grenade®, which is a Thermo Detonator, kicked into overdrive? Those two small green pills had always increased my energy levels during races, but this was off the chart.

It felt like the distances between mile markers was shorter. Miles 8, 9, and 10, all seemed to go by as if I was riding a bike. At the 11th mile water station, I felt I needed to practice taking on water, which seems daft, but I was thinking about the marathon. Knowing I was going to walk through stations to rehydrate and conserve energy during the marathon, I felt I should take this opportunity to practice. It may have been the fact that I wanted to walk and 'practicing' was just my way of justifying having a rest. During this walk through the water station at mile 11, something happened that shook me to the core because, it was at this point that the 02:30 pacer passed me.

'02:30 pacer?' I said out loud, confused.

It then sunk in and I thought,

'Does that mean I am on a 02:30 finishing pace?'

Finishing a half marathon in 2 hour and 30 minutes? Impossible! My quickest time to date was 02:52:17 at the 2015 North Lincolnshire Half Marathon. I poured the rest of the water in the bottle I was holding over my head and was now in pursuit. I thought if I could get in front of the 02:30 pacer I could break the 02:30 threshold.

Within 10 minutes of this chase, the only thing that broke, was my spirit. My body once again systematically shut down; my breathing became heavy, my feet sore, and, finally, my legs felt like stumps. The pace runner was now out of sight and the idea of a sub 02:30 half marathon became a pipedream. With every fibre of my being I tried to increase the pace for the final mile in the way I usually do, but to no avail. I believe the reason for this shutdown was once again due to my starting off too fast; damn you race day atmosphere and adrenalin! With this being said, there was a positive that could be taken from this race; I crossed the line in a respectable 02:38:50, which is still my half marathon PB to this day.

This run showed me that my training was working and I was able to sustain a faster speed for longer. I never returned to Silverstone to see if I could break that 02:30 barrier, as just finishing a marathon was my main priority … for now.

MILE 23

My New Favourite Running Word

The hardest week of my 16-week training plan was upon me: week 14. Week 13 was tough with a total of 34 miles, but this was it, the last week before my favourite word in running: taper. Not ever experiencing it before, all I knew was after all the miles I had put in, my taper was the time I could just put my feet up and relax. From what I read, a two-week period of tapering was essential for optimal performance on the day of the marathon, and who could argue with that?

It took me the entire week to psych myself up for this last 20-mile run, my longest run ever. I conjured up every positive thought I had; it's the last big run; I will never run this distance in training again; and I have two weeks' of relaxation taper time after today's run.

After my standard three packs of maple syrup instant porridge oats, two pieces of toast, a banana, and three glasses of water, I was out of the door at 4:30am. I started early as I knew it would take me a lot of time, and I didn't want it to take up too much of my Saturday. If I was honest, starting the run, I didn't know if I was really going to be able to do it. My mindset was to take one mile at a time and only think of one thing, as always, the finishing gantry.

I wore the exact ensemble I was going to wear on the big day, just to ensure there was no chafing, rubbing, or wardrobe malfunctions. I had never had problems with my outfits, but I followed the advice from friends, research, books, and magazines. Hope for the best, but prepare for the worst, as the saying goes.

This final run was like saying goodbye to old friends, as I passed the Co-op gas station at the end of Wakefield road at mile 8, I thought to myself, this was the last time I will be running by this. I felt the same as I ran the long downhill on Shepley Lane at mile 12, and past the Penistone Garden Centre at mile 18. I would walk, run, slog this final run until I had finished. To simulate the fuelling stations, I went into shops to get drinks and bananas (when they opened), but as my Garmin watch reached mile 20, I limped and hobbled the last 0.2 of a mile to my house. There was a fleeting moment that I thought I should continue and do 26.2 miles, just to see if I could do it, but after 6.5 hours of running I was beyond exhausted and just wanted a hot bath.

During the last week of training I clocked up 39 miles and was still alive, although barely. Knowing that for the next few weeks my miles would be limited to a total of maybe 8 to 12 miles per week, I eased into taper time, and it was wonderful. It turned out that I did a total of only 12 miles for both weeks combined, as I used that time to recover physically, emotionally, and mentally. During this down time, I would read running magazines, chat with friends for some final advice, and, of course, carbo load. I did ponder if I had done enough; I wondered whether I could really finish a marathon, and then started to doubt my fitness and ability. I soon found out what this feeling was as I saw a meme on Facebook that read, 'maranoia – the mental anxiety found in marathon runners, characterised by the irrational belief that last-minute disaster is imminent'. With four days to go, I was 100% in a state of maranoia.

After 16 weeks of training, my mother arriving from Canada, the family excited and all the personal support messages from friends and family, it was time to get this damn run over with. As we booked a hotel in Manchester to stay overnight pre-race and post-race, we packed up our Nissan Note and made our way to our favourite chain hotel: Premier Inn.

I was terrified.

MILE 24

The 2016 Manchester Marathon

On 9th April 2016, the night before the big race, I found myself wide awake at 2:30am. All I could think about, while I was lying on the king-sized Premier Inn bed, was that I needed to go to sleep, but maranoia had taken a full-throated grip. At 7:00am, the alarm went off and I sat up feeling completely sleep deprived. Once standing, I automatically started my pre-race routine that I had practiced many times before. Two packs of instant oatmeal, two bananas, a multivitamin, and vitamin C + zinc effervescent tablet dissolved in water.

Miles was waiting in the corner of the room surrounded by gels, bananas, and all of my tech bric-a-brac. It was like I was peeling Miles's skin off as I steadily put on each piece of clothing from his legs onto my legs, and from his chest and arms to mine. Everything was tested with a stretch, tug, or pull of the spandex material to once again ensure there would be no chafing or ripping. It felt like I was putting some battle armour on; each item had a place, and all items such as my watch, water bottle, music, gels, and bananas were all accessible and ready to use. With the final act of pinning my race number 8116 to the front of my Flash jersey, I was all set. The tricky bit was that all of this had to be done in stealth mode, as I didn't want to wake the family. I did get a 'Good luck luv', from Wendy in the darkness, as I removed the chain on the hotel room door and swung it open.

It had been pre-arranged that Wendy, Ross, Tasha, and my mum would meet me at the finish. I was to text Wendy when I was on my final mile and they would meet me as I crossed the finish line. It was also decided that I would make my way to the start line using an Uber. At this point, it was too early to enjoy the famous Premier Inn breakfast buffet, because it started at 8, and I was in my Uber at 7:30. I knew that even if I could indulge myself in a breakfast feast, I probably wouldn't, as all the books and many of my friends told me not to try anything new on race day. A full English breakfast before a race is definitely something I had never indulged in before a race, and I wasn't going to start now. With the family sorted, body fuelled, and on my way to the start line in an Uber, it was now time to enter the deepest focus bubble I had ever experienced in my running journey.

Sadly, once again my focus bubble did not allow me to really enjoy the moment. Would I ever learn? I got my bearings by finding the starting funnel then located a quiet area to reflect and attempt to stop myself from pacing like a caged animal as I sipped my Smart water. I didn't want to waste any energy like I did in Blackpool. The music was pounding in my ears and I was psyching myself up for probably the biggest challenge of my life.

The set-up of the marathon main area was the same as any 10K or half marathon I had run in the past: sponsor tents, charity tents, tents selling merchandise, and people milling around them. Well that's what I perceived it to be, as I was having nothing to do with any of it. I was trying to be zen, but it may have looked like I was possessed. No talking, no smiling no interaction, just stern looking and focused on the outside, but absolutely shitting myself on the inside.

I entered the starting funnel near the back, closed my eyes, and thought of the miles, the aches, the pains, the cold, the heat, the advice, the love, the support, and the sacrifices that my family and other people had made to help me get to this point. I knew this day was going to be emotional, but tearing up before the race started was something new.

'Come on, Sean! Get a grip!' I said out loud, giving myself a metaphorical slap across the face.

I quickly shook it off and went deeper into my bubble. I don't know where this focus bubble concept ever came from and why I enter it before a race. All I do know is I have missed so many wonderful things, before, during, and after a race due to the fact I was not living in the moment, which continues to be an utter shame.

Reflecting on these focus bubbles, as I write this book, they may have started back when I played Highschool American football for the Bishop Grandin Ghosts back in the late 80s to early 90s. I can vividly see myself sitting in the locker room listening to loud music entering a type of aggression bubble banging my head against a locker, with a helmet on, of course. I did this, especially, when we played the St Francis Browns. I recall that was a type of focus bubble; maybe that's where it started.

After the group aerobics warm up, the countdown began. The plan in my head was to not start off too fast. I even considered walking the first mile to ensure this did not happen. To help me not start off too quickly, I broke the race down into sections for the 5K, 10K, and half marathon times I was hoping to achieve. This was not about speed; these times would tell me whether I was running too fast. For example, I ran a comfortable 5K in 40 minutes, which meant I did not want to reach the 5K mark faster than 45 to 50 minutes, 10K no faster than 1 hour 50 minutes, and 13.1 miles no faster than 3 hours 50 minutes. On paper, this would mean that if I saved my energy during the first half, I might have enough energy during the second half to finish.

It took me 9 minutes and 10 seconds to reach the starting mat from where I was in the starting funnel. I had to keep my head up as there were a lot of people jockeying for position, but I also kept one eye on my watch to ensure I didn't go faster than a 14-minute mile. I dodged and weaved but soon found a comfortable pace and an area that I could call my own.

Just like that, 'One mile down and only 25.6 more to go', I thought to myself as I passed the one-mile flag that was perched on a sign next to the road. I had not started out too fast and I felt comfortable, strong, and determined. I took no notice of other runners, volunteers, cheering supporters, or the atmosphere: a HUGE SHAME. As I eased into a comfortable pace, so comfortable that once I passed the 5K flag, I was oblivious to what my 5K time was; I forgot to mentally log the actual time in relation to my race day plan. I didn't want to waste mental energy doing mental arithmetic, so I decided to wait until the 6-mile or 10K mark to get a clear picture of where I was on my timing plan.

I was approaching the 10K mark and celebrated a small victory; I had not stopped to walk and didn't have any aches or pains. My time was 01:35:15 as I passed the 10K or 6.2-mile point of the race. It was about 20 minutes faster than planned, so a body systems check was needed.

A body systems check was something I did during training runs. I liken it to what you would see in the classic arcade game Mortal Combat and the health bar for your fighter. This red bar would go down as your character got hit. When the health was at zero it would be 'FINISH HIM!' followed by 'FATALITY!' So, at the 10K mark, my feet, calves, knees, quads, hips, stomach, arms, shoulders, head, and my body overall was at 90% health, so there was nothing to worry about. I walked through the water stations as planned to keep hydrated; also, I had not yet taken any gels or eaten any of the bananas I was carrying.

As I was trying to focus on what was coming up in the race, my mind wasn't on the next milestone of the half marathon point. I found myself pondering the dreaded wall. Were there going to be snipers? Had I done enough training to make it past the wall? I then, instantaneously, gave myself yet another metaphorical slap across the face and uttered a modified version of a quote from one of my favourite movies, Matrix. 'There is no wall!'

My time as I arrived at the halfway point was 03:23:22, once again probably 20 minutes too fast. I was now thinking; will I have enough energy to finish? After a quick follow up body scan, feet 80%, calves 75%, knees 80%, quads 75%, hips 80%, stomach 70%, arms 75%, shoulders 70%, head 85%, overall 80%; I was still on track to finish.

At 05:00:29, I crossed the 30K or 18-mile mark; at this point I started to hurt and the pain started in my feet. They were throbbing; my feet must have swollen. It had become so painful I had to stop and loosen my laces. I did think I could run through it, but all the research and advice told me if something small was bothering you during a race, you deal with it ASAP; don't let it fester. So that's what I did, and it was great advice.

My next goal was to get to 20 miles, matching the longest distance I had ever run. I knew in my bones that if I could get to 20 miles, I would finish. I am not going to lie, I was struggling; my pace was slow and with each body scan, I knew my health was being zapped. My feet, calves, knees, quads, etc, were all about 40%, but overall, I was probably 55%. With my body at these levels, my pace began to lag. I no longer looked at my watch as my main goal was just to finish.

I had reached the 20-mile mark and found some energy reserve; this boost or second wind probably stemmed from knowing that, with each step, I was now entering unknown territory, and every step added distance to my longest run ever. My thoughts turned to that image of the finishing gantry I had used during all those training runs. However, this time, the image now included my kids, Wendy, and my Mum in sheer joyful disbelief. Their faces of amazement, joy, and happiness; I was doing this, and nobody was going to stop me!

A marshal asked me to run on the pavement for safety; I obliged and the people behind me did as well, allowing the slow-moving traffic to flow freely. My feet were now seriously throbbing again, and I was thinking of loosening my laces for the second time. My legs were also starting to scream at me.

'Hey Sean, you can stop now', they said.

My speed was faster than a walk but slower than a run, I would call it a shuffle. I quickly used up my second wind and started doubting if I could finish at all, as my body started to shut down. Was this the wall?

I returned to the road as I saw runners ahead divert back on to the closed roads. Within a half a mile of passing the 20-mile mark, my body and mind started to pack it in; it was time for a body check, feet, calves, knees, quads, hips, stomach, arms, shoulders, head, were all in single digits. I needed to dig deep and push through.

Looking ahead about 200 yards, I saw a marshal standing in the street. He was wearing a high-vis jacket, sunglasses, and was holding a radio; he looked very official. As I moved closer to him, he started to walk towards me leaving his bike and helmet behind. I assumed he wanted me to go back on the sidewalk. As I moved toward the sidewalk, he still walked towards me, which was weird. Maybe he was going to give me some words of encouragement such as,

'Well done! Only 6 miles left!'

I wish he had said that. What he did say was the last thing I wanted to hear, and pretty much the opposite of well done.

'Hi mate. I'm going to have to ask you to stop', he said in this authoritarian tone.

'Stop? Running? For how long?' I asked.

I knew that if I stopped, I would not physically be able to get started again. Plus, I could just see the two other runners ahead of me, just before they disappeared around a bend, about 500 yards ahead.

'Sorry, but I need you to stop running; we are opening the road and we can't let you run any more', he said, as if I should understand.

'Stop? For good? You mean I'm unable to finish?' I said, as I tried to process what he meant.

'Yup' he said, sheepishly.

I started to comprehend what he was saying, as the full weight of his words were processed with a two-minute delay. I then said, with an astonished lilt in my voice,

'So, you are telling me that 16 weeks of training and over 350 miles was all for nothing?'

'Sorry', he said.

I even tried playing the guilt card, by begging,

'Please, my mum came in from Canada to see me finish; my kids and wife are waiting? Is there really nothing you can do?'

Stone faced, not really knowing what this really meant to me, the volunteer marshal replied,

'Nope, we are opening the road and it would be too dangerous.'

'I'll run on the pavement!' I pleaded.

'Sorry, this next bit doesn't have a pavement, and we have to open the roads', he said as if he wanted this conversation to end.

'Am I the first you stopped?'

'Yup, we just opened the road, sorry.'

This conversation ended as he turned his back on me and walked off.

In that moment, the image of the finishing gantry evaporated in my mind. I then became emotional as with only six miles to go, my marathon dream was over. I was told that a bus would pick me up to take me to the finish. The finish, where my kids, Wendy, and my mum were waiting. How was I going to explain this?

As my focus bubble popped and I admitted defeat, I thought stopping people at this point seemed strategic as it was outside a Premier Inn, and a good place to corral people to wait for a bus that would shuttle us to the finish. I limped into the parking lot and sat dejected on a cold brick wall, wondering how to word a text to Wendy. I looked up from my phone to see other runners who were behind me getting the same speech. I was too far away to hear full sentences, but knowing body language as I do, it looked as if people were having the same response and conversations I had just experienced. After about 30 minutes, there were more than10 people all feeling sorry for themselves, sitting on this wall. No words were exchanged, but no words needed to be said. It was over for all of us.

Finally finding the words to send to Wendy in a text, I pressed send. At the same moment a fox and a chicken were stopped by the same marshal who stopped the rest of us. I thought I may have been hallucinating, but it was two women dressed in fancy dress with their numbers pinned to the outside of their costumes. When they were told of the situation their body language was different than any of us rejected ones. They weren't having it, and the fox was letting the marshal know by yelling. Yelling so loud I could hear snippets of what was being said. The fox was more resolute than the chicken.

I could hear the fox yelling statements such as,

'You can't stop me, I have every right to walk on these roads!'

'This is bullshit, we are going to finish!'

'Let's just go!'

The marshal seemed to have met his match, but he still tried to stand his ground.

'It's too dangerous to continue on the roads.'

'I am going to need your number, if you're going to continue.'

The chicken handed over her number quite quickly and seemed to be afraid to break the rules, which I thought was ironic. The fox had continued walking and saw what was happening; she then quickly walked back to the marshal and snatched the number back saying,

'We paid for these; they're ours!'

The fox grabbed the chicken by the hand and continued walking beside the cars on the road.

The last thing I heard was the marshal yelling, 'You're not going to get a time!'

I was thinking, should I have done that? Should I have stood my ground and said,

'To hell with you, I'm going to finish this damn race.'

I was truly inspired; I felt like yelling,

'HELL YEAH! YOU GO GIRL! FIGHT THE POWER!'

For a fleeting moment, as the surge of adrenalin hit me, I wanted to try and catch up with them and in solidarity, finish the run together, but reality set in. My legs were like stones and even if I could muster up the strength and courage, if I didn't catch up with them quickly, how would I know where to go? Would the other route marshals still be there? I quickly dismissed this idea and retreated under my dark cloud. I wondered how I was going to explain this to my family and supporters. I felt like an utter failure; I'd let everybody down.

Now on the bus, some were looking at the funny side; some were emotional; some were relieved; and others, like me, were reflecting on what could have been. All I posted on Facebook was, 'stopped at 20 miles for running too slow, with only six miles to go **#devastated**.' Within 15 seconds, likes, wows, angry faces, and comments were flying in as people were actually waiting to hear about my progress on the day and were wondering how I was getting on. I didn't have the energy to read or reply to any of these condolences.

It was about a 27-minute ride to the finish area. As the bus found a good place to park, I still didn't really know what to say to Wendy, the kids, or my mum. As I got off the bus, the very first thing that I saw was the finish gantry. It looked exactly as the image that I had burnt into my brain for the last 16 weeks. The only thing that was different was the perspective. From where we were, the finish area was behind a large chain-linked fence. The bus dropped us off in a parking area and was separate from where the action was happening. All I noticed was how dirty it was; banana peels, tin foil runners' blankets, empty water, and Lucozade bottles all swirling in the wind. The area seemed dank, cold, and full of despair, probably because I was feeling the same way.

The first thing I did was throw my number in the overflowing rubbish bin. I then walked to the new pre-arranged meeting point that Wendy and I had set via text. The look on my kids' faces almost set me off again, but the hug from Wendy and my mum helped. I explained everything that happened as we looked for a way back to the hotel. I tried to put on an optimistic persona, but inside I wished the ground would have just swallowed me up.

Once home, settled, and in the process of recovering physically and mentally, I did do a rant on Facebook about what happened. I then reposted my rant on all Manchester Marathon social media platforms. Once that was out of my system, I deleted all email marathon correspondence, pictures, training updates, I ripped up the training plan that was on my fridge, I even deleted the run from Strava. If it's not on Strava, it never happened.

If I am honest, this was probably the hardest chapter to write, not because it brought back bad memories, but because I have no real memory or evidence of this race at all. I really had to dig deep into my memory bank to piece it all together. Supported by a quick Google search, I did find the only piece of evidence that I even ran this race. I found the Did Not Finish (DNF) results on the 2019 Manchester Marathon race page's archived results.

If the same situation happened again, could I have done what the fox did? Would I have the balls to throw caution to the wind, stand my ground, and with reckless abandon, disobey event staff, and finish? All I can say is that the fox became a hero to me on that day. The punchline to this joke was, as a comment on the rant I posted on Facebook, a friend of mine posted the finishing picture of the chicken and the fox crossing the finish line with their arms raised in victory and a gun time of 07:31:56. In the picture, the finishing gantry was in full display. Thanks Gareth (salt meets wound).

Ummm. What Marathon?

MILE 25

What Now?

During the weeks following the race 'that shall not be named', I was in a bit of a self-imposed shame spiral. Running was not something I wanted to do or even thought about. Weeks were filled with watching movies and reflective walks, but no running. It did take me just over three weeks to lace up my shoes and go for a proper run.

While running, the first thing that struck me was my lack of motivation. Even within the first few strides the image of the finishing gantry returned. All I remember thinking was, 'Been there, done that, and failed'. I needed something to train for, something new to visualise.

With the run over and a quick search of upcoming events, I found some races of a distance that I knew I could do: the 2016 North Lincolnshire Half Marathon and the 2016 Rock 'n' Roll Liverpool Half Marathon. I even considered attempting the Liverpool Marathon to try and redeem my self-worth, but looking closer, the idea evaporated with the words 'cut off time', which seemed to jump out at me from the terms and conditions and smack me in the face.

As a backdrop to all my self-loathing, there was one thing that I could look forward to – a five-week trip to Canada for the entire summer of 2016. Not only was it an opportunity to catch up with my family and friends, it was also an opportunity to leave the kids with their Yiayia and Papou. (Greek for grandmother and grandfather) while Wendy and I did our own thing. This trip also opened the door for me to run a race in my home country. So, this begged the question – could I enter a race while in Canada and add international runner to my running CV? Answer, why not?

With yet another Google search, I found some 5K and 10K races, but what jumped out at me was the 2016 Edmonton Half Marathon on 21st August. Now, nothing could be finalised at this point as our Canadian visits were usually filled with family gatherings, planned trips, and more family gatherings, so I didn't want to commit and disrupt the pre-arranged UK Kachmarski's tour schedule.

Following some intense negotiation with my mum, and a tweak of her timetable, I officially entered the 2016 Edmonton Half Marathon. Brilliant. Something to focus on and look forward to. The cloud of funk was starting to lift.

With some races now firmly on my calendar and a new-found enthusiasm for running, I, once again, started to clog people's social networking feeds with my upcoming race announcements, training selfies, and GPS Strava route maps. One of my updates caught the eye of my cousin, Paul Andrews.

I have four cousins, Sam, Patti, Chris, and Paul, all of whom I have always treated as brothers and a sister growing up, and I still do. Our times together were filled with love, laughs, and cut-throat banter. They are all very successful in their own right with two of my cousins being well-established doctors (Sam and Chris), one well respected chiropractor (Patti), and an IT Genius working for a large company (Paul). With this being said, when it came to my cousins and me, there are two things celebrated throughout the family and beyond. One, it was well known that even though my cousins had the brains,

I had the looks; two, I was always known as the favourite grandchild. **#micdrop**.

One of Paul's replies to my avalanche of Facebook updates was, 'Why don't you run the Edmonton Marathon, instead of the half?' After throwing up a bit in my mouth, I replied 'NOPE!'

MILE 26

Harmonic Convergence

Nope, not again, and no chance were my censored thoughts on the subject of running another marathon. My marathon scab was still in the process of healing and I didn't want to start picking at it. It took me a few days just to decompress from the mere thought of trying again.

Next to my American football days, many, many, many years ago, I was currently in the best shape of my life. I knew this because when I tried to convince fellow beginner runners to have a go at running a half marathon with me, I found myself saying,

'It's only 13.1 miles!'

'ONLY 13.1 miles?!' would always be the reply.

No 16-week training schedule was needed to train for a half marathon, and I could even attend half marathon races with only four or five days' notice. My thoughts of just finishing changed to wanting to break three-hour half marathons or bettering a PB for shorter races. It was not until this moment that I realised that it was the challenge, and not the running, which kept me motivated. I then thought, 'What would be more challenging than attempting a second marathon? Could Paul be on to something?' With this mindset, I sat down and looked at a calendar using the logical or frontal part of my brain and not the limbic or emotional part. I mapped out the logistics of a potential second attempt in Canada, and, at first glance, things looked promising.

As it was nearing the end of April, I figured that if I started a new 16-week training plan on 2nd May, and we flew to Canada the week of 25th July, with the race being held on 21st August, when I landed in Calgary, my taper period would start. Trust me, if you saw it visually on a calendar, it made perfect sense. Fate seemed to have taken control of my journey.

This meant that all the miles; hard work; and the blood, sweat, and tears, would be tackled while I was still in the UK. I could still get a few miles in while tapering in Canada. Ultimately, I knew that trips to Canada wouldn't be too taxing, as my parents pretty much cater to my every whim when I return home. Adding to this revelation and train of thought, my entire family could potentially be at the finish line cheering me on. Add to that having some down time to recover post-race while my mum and dad took the kids on different day trips, it seemed like a no brainer. All the planets were aligning and the universe was daring me to do it all over again.

Then, reality set in, with the wasted training of my failed event still fresh in my mind I wasn't sure I wanted to put myself, let alone my family, through that again. Even as I was processing the fact that I was thinking about doing it all again, it did actually seem logical. I was currently still marathon fit, so the weeks of training should be easier than before. If I could find a way to maintain my fitness, maybe I wouldn't need to train as much. My logical brain then went into overdrive and every negative thought was countered with a positive rebuttal. A pros and cons list was then created, something my mum always told me to do if I ever had a big decision. The pros outnumbered the cons by almost three to one. Could it be possible that I just talked myself into attempting another 26.2 miles? As my last marathon attempt wasn't on Strava, technically, it never happened, so ultimately the answer to that question was a very nervous yes. So, with a weirdly timed long-distance phone call to the Edmonton marathon event team, due to the difference in time zones, I paid the difference of $17 to swap my half marathon entry for a marathon entry, thus starting the process that I said that I would never do again.

MILE 27

Will I join the 1% club?

The date for the start of my new training schedule, 2nd May, came round quickly, and before I knew it, my daily mileage started to populate the new 16-week marathon training plan that I, once again, Blu-tacked to the fridge for motivation. With each run, the image of a new finishing gantry appeared; this time, it was with my family waiting to embrace me as I finished. My first attempt was soon a distant memory, and with each step, I gained more confidence in my ability to finish my second attempt at a Marathon. Before I knew it, and with absolutely no record of the Manchester marathon anywhere, in my head, the Edmonton Marathon became my first attempt.

During my first week of training, I logged 25 miles; in the second week, 24; and third week, 22. I just wanted to maintain my fitness and not peak too early. With the excitement of a trip to Canada that resonated throughout our household, my training continued with 34 miles logged in week 11; 31 miles logged in week 12; and 29 miles logged in week 13. I peaked with a 23-mile run (my longest run ever), just two days before we departed for Calgary and the warm embrace from my parents. The first two weeks in Canada would not only be family time; they would also be an opportunity for me to enjoy my favourite part of training – taper time.

The weeks seemed to fly by; was it our eagerness and enthusiasm we always felt when we knew we were flying to Canada? Or was it over 350 miles of running that filled all my time and thoughts? My guess was that it was a combination of both. On the Saturday of week 13, Wendy, Ross, Tasha, and I were all packed and ready to go. As Jim, our usual taxi guy, arrived to pick us up to take us to Manchester airport, I found myself wondering: when I return to the UK, will I have joined the 1% of the population who have finished a marathon?

PTT = 6.5 + 5.5 + 3.5 + 1 = 16.5 mi · X = ROTATE IN NEW SHOES.

My 16 Week Edmonton Marathon Training Plan

August 21st, 2016

Week	Mon	Tues	Weds	Thurs	Fri	Sat	Sun	Total	Real Total
1: May 2nd	REST	6 miles	3 miles	3 miles	REST	12 miles	REST	24 miles	25
2: May 9th	REST	3 miles	6 miles	REST	REST	REST	North Lyncs Half	22 miles	23.5
3: May 16th	REST	REST	6 miles	3 miles	REST	12 miles	REST	21 miles	21.5
3: May 23rd	REST	6 miles	3 miles	REST	REST	REST	Liverpool Half	22 miles	25
5: May 30th	REST	REST	6 miles	3 miles	REST	12 miles	REST	21 miles	13.5
6: June 6th	2 miles	REST	6 miles	6 miles	REST	13 miles	REST	27 miles	25
7: June 13th	2 miles	2 miles	6 miles	3 miles	REST	14 miles	REST	26 miles	27
8: June 20th	2 miles	2 miles	6 miles	3 miles	REST	13 miles	REST	26 miles	23.5 (HFW)
9: June 27th	2 miles	2 miles	6 miles	3 miles	REST	16 miles	REST	28 miles	15
10: July 4th	2 miles	6 miles	10 miles	REST	REST	18 miles	REST	28 miles	29
11: July 11th	2 miles	3 miles	6 miles	REST	REST	18 miles	REST	29 miles	34
12: July 18th	REST	3 miles	6 miles	6 miles	REST	20 miles	REST	35 miles	31
13: July 25th	REST	6 miles	2 miles	REST	REST	ER 20 miles	Fly to Canada	28 miles	29
14: Aug 1st	REST	REST	2 miles	5 miles	REST	2 miles	REST	12 miles	16.5
15: Aug 8th	REST	[illegible]	[illegible]	[illegible]	REST	2 miles	REST	12 miles	7
16: Aug 15th	REST	2 miles	REST	REST	REST	REST	Race Weekend		30.7

Notes

Notes

392.7 MILES
632 KM

This was the training plan I created to record my miles for the Edmonton Marathon. It was on my fridge as a reminder of what I had done and what I needed to do. Having it on Strava was good, but seeing it daily for motivation was better.

MILE 28

Maranoia: The Sequel

Seeing my parents at the Calgary International airport is always joyous. I always revert back to being a kid when I hug my mum and dad after a long time away. There are no words that I can use to express how much I love them; they have always been there for me through the good times and the bad. I wish I was a poet; I would then be able to put my true feeling across about just how much they mean to me. However, I have noticed that, since the grandkids were born, my arrival embraces have got shorter!

'As parents, we want our children to be successful at whatever challenges they choose for themselves. We are so proud of Sean for choosing running as a vehicle to better his health, perseverance, and achievement of his goals. It hasn't all been easy or without disappointment, but through it all he has shown us his courage and strength.' ~ ***Celia*** *and* ***Ron Kachmarski***

Being back in Calgary always feels like a king-sized 13.5 tog duvet: warm, comfortable, protected, and safe. As I am now so used to driving on the left-hand side of the road in the UK, I don't drive in Calgary. This gives me the opportunity to be amazed at all of the changes that have occurred to my home city, as I watch it go by, sitting in the back seat of my mum's car, responding blissfully to the usual questions,

'How was your flight?'

'Was the flight full?'

With these flight-based questions out of the way, the queries then turned towards what I needed to prepare for my epic run. I knew my parents were proud of this attempt as they asked me what I needed to help with my prep,

'What food do you need?'

'Are you going to do any long runs? '

'When do you want to leave for Edmonton?'

With it now being taper time, my prep runs were flexible and *definitely* not long. I told my parents that I would like to be in Edmonton a few days before the race as I wanted to enjoy the atmosphere of the entire weekend and not just that of the race day.

With regards to food, I didn't want to eat anything too exotic or out of the ordinary, but I knew that some foods that I usually eat while in Canada will not have been on my menu for quite some time. The usual Greek dolmades, Greek melomakarona, Ukrainian sauerkraut perogies, cabbage rolls, and my all-time favourite, my dad's New York 3-inch thick strip barbeque loin steak with peppercorn sauce, set on top of a large piece of garlic bread and topped off with a generous portion of cheesy mash. Just writing about it makes my mouth water and reminds me of a UK M&S advert. All of that delicious food unfortunately would have to be put on hold until after the race. I just didn't want to take the risk of shocking my system with foods I had not eaten since my last visit over two years ago. Let the maranoia begin!

International running was new to me and I felt the best way to combat jet lag was to tackle it head on with a few miles on the afternoon of our arrival. It seemed to work, but I was in a bit of a shock as halfway through this light run, I found it hard to breathe and my chest started to hurt. Not a constricting pain like I had seen in heart attack awareness commercials, just an ache. It felt like my lungs had shrunk and I had to take shorter breaths. What the hell was going on? As I couldn't even finish a 2-mile easy run, I started to worry. Then it hit me, I had completely overlooked elevation and running at altitude. I thought that was only for international athletes preparing for the Olympics.

With a quick Google search, I found that the Wakefield area in which I ran my 400 miles of training, was at an elevation of 43 meters (141 feet) above sea level, Calgary is 1,048 meters (3,438 feet) above sea level. This revelation only added to my maranoia; was I going to be ready? How long would it take for my body to get used to this altitude? I didn't want to run a lot of miles during my taper but I wasn't really sure what to do. During week 14, I did 17 miles, which seemed to get rid of my chest ache. During week 15, I only did 7 miles, which was glorious.

MILE 29

673

Everything was set, we were to travel to Edmonton after a final family meal at my parent's house. At this last supper, most of my cousins were there, along with a few of my parents' friends who came to wish me well. The weekend was jam packed with activities but I had it all committed to memory:

On the Friday, there was a Sports Running Expo at which I wanted to buy some marathon merchandise. It was also an opportunity to pick up my number, shirt, and goody bag. My cousin, Heidi (Paul's wife), had entered the half marathon as a walker and we signed our kids up for the Kids 1K fun run, to be held on the Saturday.

Edmonton's Running Festival Schedule:

Saturday:

Kids 1K fun run

Sunday:

6:00am Marathon Walk
7:00am Marathon Run

8:00am Half Marathon Run
10:30am 10K Run
11:30am 5K Run

Following a gut-busting meal that consisted of all the foods that I vowed to stay away from before the race, but was too damn good to just watch people eat, the talk returned to the topic of the marathon. Paul mentioned that they had a record number of entries for the event this year. 'GREAT!' I thought. I was pretty sure there would not be as many runners as that of the Great North Run, which had over 50,000 participants, but I thought it might be close. I then remembered, in all the excitement of changing from the half to the full marathon, that I had forgotten my golden rule – always check the number of runners in the previous year's event and find out what the slowest time was.

'673', Paul said, nonchalantly.

Now, when Steven Spielberg does make this book into a movie, I suggest he uses a dolly zoom cinematic effect here, as all the blood drained from my face and a tidal wave of disbelief, fear, and WTF hit me like a MAC or Eddie Stobart truck.

'WHAT?!' I shrieked, spitting out and almost choking on the bits of watermelon I had in my mouth.

With his head down, reading off his phone, not seeing me convulse in disbelief, Paul repeated,

'Ya, 673 runners in the marathon this year; almost a record.'

'673?? You are joking?' I said, hoping it was a cruel cousin wind-up.

I then started to panic.

'Well I'm going to be last for sure, and worse, maybe even stopped.'

In all of my past races, it never bothered me being last, but this was different; I was going to be last by hours. After this shocking news, I investigated it further. The average finish time of the 2015 Edmonton Marathon was 04:12:18. In any online marathon time predicting formula or app I used, my predicted finishing time was going to be between 6.5 and 7.5 hours. I was deflated and on the brink of throwing the towel in.

I couldn't sleep that night; my only thought was that I now had 673 reasons to pull out of the race; I was going to be humiliated. In a desperate attempt, the next morning I called the event team, and asked if I could start with the Marathon walkers, who were going to start an hour earlier. They said, unfortunately, walkers had a different race number and colour, and if they were seen running, they would be disqualified. I pleaded my 'slow poke' case, but to no avail.

Snippets of my Manchester marathon debacle returned into my conscious memory as a painful flickering montage. I was now at a crossroads: pull out and disappoint the family, and throw away my training, or be humiliated by making all the event staff and volunteers wait that extra few hours for me to finish. That is, if they did wait. I now had visions of me coming to the end of the race and seeing the finishing gantry being dismantled, with all the medals packed away. All of my Doomsday scenarios were going through my mind. The kicker was, as Edmonton is a 3-hour drive from my hometown, I had a long time to really dwell on my conundrum.

MILE 30

Come Hell or High Water, I AM Going to Finish a Marathon

I decided to give it a go, do my best, run as far as I could, and get the job done. Negative thoughts tried to enter my consciousness but were dismissed just as quickly. It was my family who brought me through to the other side along with the comments from far and wide on Facebook. I was also determined not to waste all the time and sacrifices I'd made during my 16-week training schedule. I made a conscious effort to hold off on entering my 'focus bubble' too early, as I really wanted to enjoy this experience, despite it being tainted.

The day before the big race was all about the kids and their 1K fun run. Knowing that both Ross and Tasha were willing to take part in such an event felt like an achievement in itself. The whole family were there, cheering for all the young kids, nieces, nephews, brothers, and sisters running the 1K race with the reward of a hefty medal for their effort. I like to think that their participation in such an event was partly due to my efforts and commitment to my own cause.

At the start of my journey, I made a point not to touch any marathon medals until I got my own, so it was difficult not to touch the medal the kids had received; it was the same as the one I would get after my 26.2-mile slog.

With the kids happy with their achievement, the discussion turned to what the adults were going to do tomorrow on race day: the best places to watch, where to be and when, and guesstimating my predicted finishing time. My initial thought was that my family wanted to know this information because they were worried about being swept up in the exciting atmosphere of the Marathon weekend and thought they might miss me finishing. This could not be further from the truth. They wanted to know my predicted finishing time so they wouldn't show up at the finishing line too early and have to spend time waiting. It was just a polite way of saying that they wanted to spend more time in bed before waiting for something that may, in fact, never happen: me finishing.

I announced that I hoped to finish my first marathon in 7 hours. My running coach, Coach Google, helped me come up with this prediction. To predict a rough marathon finishing time, Google told me to take my average half marathon time, double it and add an hour. My average half marathon was 3 hours, so I doubled it (6 hours) and add an hour (7 hours). 'Whoop! There it is, my finishing goal', I said to myself. However, I did also announce a different finishing scenario,

'If I get stopped at the fifth hour for running too slow, I'll text ya.'

This caveat was always at the tail end of every sentence when I discussed my predicted finishing time.

MILE 31

2016 Edmonton Marathon, GULP!

Even though there were only 673 runners in this race, it seemed like a lot more. The 10K runners, half marathon walkers, half marathon runners, and, of course, the full marathon nut jobs were all in the same area doing light sprints, taking selfies, stretching, and lining up for the Portaloo. This number of people at the start was what I was used to and the atmosphere was electric. With all this being said, today's atmosphere seemed slightly different but I could not put my finger on it until I realised that I hadn't entered my 'focus bubble' yet. For such a big event, the old Sean would have entered his 'focus bubble' when the plane landed in Canada. I was truly in the moment and it was a bit weird. I didn't know how the day was going to end; all I knew was that, by the end of the day, I truly believed I was going to be a marathon runner.

It started like any other race; we were crowded like battery chickens in the starting funnel, slowly walking to the start line, pressing the button on my GPS watch as I stepped on the timing mat, followed by the standard double chest tap with my fist and a point to the sky, to once again say thanks to everybody who got me here. I was off.

Relaxed is not a word I usually use to describe my running, yet I got into a groove early and felt comfortable with my pace, cadence, foot strike, and posture. I didn't know what most of those terms meant, but I was feeling good. For the first mile, I clocked myself at 00:15:32, mentally ticking off my mini achievement I had set for my self during my pre-race sleepless night, which was not to start off too fast. I then eased into a pace of 13- to 14-minute miles – so far so good.

With songs such as, *Let's Get Ridiculous* by Redfoo and *Thunderstruck the Hardforze Remix* by Platinum Deejayz reverberating my ear drums, my pace quickened to about 12-minute miles until I noticed this and, subsequently, slowed down. The first 10 to 12 miles were standard as my body was now used to this distance, but I was holding back slightly, as I knew what was coming.

At 12 miles, the first thing that came to my mind was that I was almost halfway; this called for a now classic systems check, Legs 80%, stomach 90%, arms and shoulders 80%, head 85%, overall 85% – right on track. As I approached the half marathon mark, which was the end of a loop back into the Edmonton Downtown area, there was a lady just in front of me who seemed to be struggling. As I passed her, I noticed she had a different coloured race bib; she was a marathon walker and had started an hour ahead of the marathon runners. She was red in the face and looked like the end of her journey was close at hand. I couldn't see her continuing in the state she was in. I slowed my pace and asked if she was ok; her reply was nonverbal. She gave me a look that I liken to any group of people being chased in a slow-moving zombie chase scene; she just looked at me as if to say,

'Save yourself; this is as far as I am going to go.'

I gave her an extra water bottle that I'd hoarded from the last water station, and said

'Well done; you should be proud of how far you've come'

Following that statement, I crossed the half marathon line at 03:15:23; it was quicker than I wanted but I felt ok.

At this point, I knew I was last and realised that all the supporters, diehard volunteers and staff would now be waiting for me to finish before they could pack up and go home. The finishing gantry was now behind me as the race essentially became an out and back. That's is all I had left to finish, a 13.1-mile out and back.

On the road adjacent to me, I could see people filled with emotion and exuberance as they finished their races. Most were finishing half marathons but there were a few quicksilvers who were finishing a marathon. I turned to a group of volunteers cheering me on at the halfway mark and said,

'See you in four hours!' I think they thought I was joking.

The runner's high of passing the halfway mark very quickly turned into a shame spiralling low. I noticed my current pace was a 16-minute mile; I was slowing down – slowing way down. I just could not get my legs to move any faster and my energy started to drain. Was this a wall? A lack of training? A marathon curse? I was in trouble – deep trouble. It was such a quick turn of events that shook me the most, from feeling and running so well to being physically and emotionally exhausted within minutes.

My body was just not responding to what my head was telling it to do. I would only describe my running stride as a shuffle. I knew if I walked, I would keep walking, or, even worse, stop. With a water station ahead, I knew it was an opportunity to get some water, shake it off, dig deep, and get this done.

I approached the Ravine Drive and 138 street water station knowing that I needed to shake this feeling of dread, and somehow find the energy to finish. I approached a sea of green shirts – the volunteers giving up their time to support us weary runners. I always thank the volunteers when I pass water stations; without them, events like this would not happen. Like a footballer at the end of a match, I clapped my hands above my head and yelled,

'THANKS FOR VOLUNTEERING!'

I grabbed some water bottles and restocked two of the three pouches on the back of my Flash cycling shirt, turned up my music, and visualised the finishing gantry. My focus bubble reengaged.

About 400 feet past the water station, I was joined by a guy in a green shirt, one of the volunteers from the water station. I thought I had dropped something and he was returning it to me. He spoke, but I did not hear him. Annoyed I took my headphone off and said,

'Hi?'

'Can I run with you for a bit?' the volunteer asked, enthusiastically.

'Umm, if you like.' I said in between breaths, returning my earphone over my ear.

He spoke again, 'I will run with you for a mile, if that's ok.'

'What?' I said, reluctantly removing my earphone from my right ear, again.

'I will run with you for a bit if that's ok', he repeated with even more enthusiasm

'OK' I said, 'But I am not much of a talker when I run.'

'That's ok, you're doing great', he replied, becoming just a random guy and not a volunteer anymore, in my mid-run haze.

This guy continued to talk while I was running and I was torn. I just wanted to be left alone to listen to my music, but this guy had found the courage to approach and encourage a perfect stranger who looked like he was struggling. After about 1,000 feet of hearing this guy's muffled words, I took my headphones off for the last time and asked him his name.

'Rene', he said.

'My name is Sean. Thanks for running with me', I said between the heavy breathing.

'No problem; I think it's brilliant that you're running a marathon. You're doing so well', Rene said.

We exchanged pleasantries but Rene did most of the talking for the next 2 miles. I gave him the short version of my running journey to date and he would reply with words that you would hear from a coach or cheerleader: Wow! Great! That's fantastic! You should be proud! Well done!

Rene was wearing cargo shorts and a baseball cap that he would swap between wearing the peak at the front, then at the back. He was also wearing canvas shoes a bit like retro Converse All Stars. I thought to myself that they were not running shoes and I bet they were uncomfortable to run in. His running speed was that awkward pace between a walk and a light jog, but that was down to my slog pace as he stuck by my side encouraging me in every step that I took.

We were probably at the 19-mile mark when a runner passed me. I was in a bit of shock as I thought I was last. I then remembered thinking,

'Well if I wasn't last then, I'm definitely last now.'

But I didn't care at this point; I just wanted to finish.

Rene continued to chat, mostly encouragement, but to fill the silence, he soon opened up to me about his life, what he had done, where he came from and his family, which was a nice distraction between the running/walking that we did. There is a rule in running that I am not sure is universal, but I would like to think that it is: 'what is said on a run, stays on the run.'

Rene went into some issues he was facing in his life and how he was coping with them.

During a pause in his story, my mind returned to the finishing gantry and I said out loud,

'Where the hell is this turnaround point?'

'Oh, it's up by that stop sign, ahead', Rene replied with confidence.

There was so much confidence in his voice that I thought he knew for sure. But, when I got to that stop sign, he said,

'Not this one, that one up ahead.'

It took me until the fifth time, when Rene again said,

'Not this one, that one up ahead', that I realised that he really didn't know.

It became a bit of a joke; every time we passed a stop sign, I would say sarcastically,

'Is this the one?' And we would both laugh.

My legs were sore and I kept grabbing my quadriceps to massage them. I was moving at a snail's pace when I started to doubt I would finish. I was still moving away from the finish line; the road ahead seemed long and undulating and with its turns and curves, the turnaround point could have been close but, right now, it was nowhere to be seen. I was hurting and I was only at 19 miles, I had not even reached my personal distance record of 23 miles; hell I had not even reached the 20 miles I got to in Manchester. In-between the thoughts of 'how the hell am I going to finish this damn race' and Rene's relentless encouragement, we hit the turnaround point, which was, thankfully, closer than I thought. HUZZAH!

Every step I was taking was now a step closer to the finish, but I was flagging, and, with every step, my legs were burning with pain. Rene must have clocked this as his encouragement went into overdrive. With time seeming to slow, we found ourselves at the water station at which Rene joined me. His plan had been to stop here but we now had this 'finish together' connection going on. Confirming this unspoken partnership, Rene asked if he could finish the race with me; I said yes. He ran ahead to make some arrangements as I am sure his car, friends he may have come with, and a pickup in the centre of the Edmonton Downtown area needed to be explained, negotiated, and arranged. That was assuming we made it that far.

With everything explained and the group of volunteers informed, the amount of cheering that I heard as I approached the water station was overwhelming. Clapping, yelling, shouting, smiles, and words of encouragement were all directed at me; I was completely taken aback. I sheepishly grabbed some water, said thanks, and increased my pace to show my gratitude. Within 100 yards of me passing the water station, Rene was back at my side.

'You are doing so well; you should be proud.'

With all the excitement over, I looked at my GPS watch; it read 20 miles, so 6 miles (10K) left. I told Rene my Manchester Marathon story.

'You will finish this race, Sean; I've got your back!' Rene said with conviction.

I just wish I had his optimism at this point; my legs were like stumps. They were sore and, with every step, they got worse. I tried everything. Visualising the start of a 10K run from my home; visualising the finish gantry; and thinking of my family at the finish. I had already dug deep and I had no energy left to dig any deeper. I tried to think positively and had a quick word with myself; how could I stop now, with only 6 miles left?

Just ahead, there were a group of hard-core marathon supporters, still waiting for the last runner. There were 12 adults and 8 kids milling around. I was feeling sluggish, pained, and on empty. The cheers and support from this group were awe-inspiring. As we passed, this group of kids started to run with us; I felt like Rocky Balboa. It was at this point that I felt the gravity of what I was doing and started to get emotional. There was no way I was stopping now.

'See, everybody is behind you, Sean. You're going to do this, I believe in you', Rene shouted.

My pace slowed again as the excitement of the group had passed, and volunteers on bikes had now joined us. I feared that they were going to tell me to stop, like in Manchester. This time it was the opposite of what happened in Manchester. They asked me if I needed anything, gels, food, water? I just said, 'no thanks', and continued slogging. After about 10 minutes of toiling, I stopped dead in my tracks and with no forward motion or explanation, I announced,

'That's it, my run is over. I'm done; I'm stopping.'

The look on Rene's and the bike riders' faces was that of astonishment and disbelief.

'Just joking', I said, and started to grind it out again.

The look on Rene's face was priceless. We all had a laugh, which was followed by a huge sigh of relief from Rene. Soon after this tomfoolery, the unspoken question was still hanging in the air – could I finish this damn race?

Those 6 miles turned into 5 miles and those 5 miles turned into 4 miles. Rene was there every step of the way encouraging me, pushing me, supporting me. If I needed water, he would run ahead to the next water station and get my water bottle filled and bring it back to me. If I ate a banana or granola bar, Rene would snatch the rubbish from me and put it in the bin on the side of the road. I honestly felt every word out of Rene's mouth was genuine and I now wanted us to finish this race together. I could see the downtown skyline and knew the end was near.

At 23 miles, I told Rene that every step I took now was a step further than the longest distance I had ever run. There were 3.6 miles left (just over 5K); a parkrun – easy, right? NO, my legs were the issue now; would I be able to stand, let alone run, anymore. With every step, the muscles in my legs ached and I felt extreme, excruciating pain. I was weaving from side to side on the park path, wincing. As we were exiting the park and moving from the path onto the downtown main street asphalt, it happened.

At the park's exit there were 10 people in green shirts; volunteers who waited all this time to support the last runner. As I passed them, they cheered like I was winning the race. Seeing and hearing this, I broke down. The wave of emotion was overwhelming; the gratitude I felt turned to tears of joy and pain. It hit me like a megaton nuclear explosion from out of nowhere. I covered my face, bawling; it was proper loud crying and as I was breathing so hard I was having to gulp for air to breathe – gulp crying. I couldn't even get the words out to say thank you; I was a wreck. For the moment, this intense crying took my mind off the pain I was feeling.

Downtown Edmonton still had all the roads closed off for the marathon. With only 2 miles left, I had Rene, two bike riders, and now a police car following me with its lights flashing. 'WOW!' I though. 'A police escort!' As the gulp crying was now intermittent, Rene told me I could walk if I wanted to. At the time I thought that his request was weird, as I was going to finish this race running. It then occurred to me that as Rene knew my goal was to finish under 7 hours, he calculated this goal was achievable if we just moved a bit faster. The strange request stemmed from the fact Rene deduced that my walk was now faster than my run.

As it was a busy road, the intersections had cars backed up for blocks maybe even miles. I slowed my pace, which was not difficult, to run beside the police car.

'Please open up the roads. I can run on the sidewalk', I pleaded to the police officer who had been following me for a while now.

He looked back at me with a steely stare, and from behind his tinted aviator glasses, he pointed at me and said,

'You got this!'

We then entered one of the large backed up intersections. My head was down in embarrassment, ensuring I didn't make eye contact with any of the drivers. I heard yelling and honking. I was so uncomfortable, ashamed, mortified, and nervous. I looked up to mouth the words, 'I'm sorry', but what I actually saw was people yelling, screaming, and honking in support.

'Go Flash, Go! Keep going! Well done!' (cue the return of more intense gulp crying.)

All this time, Rene continued his words of support; I really didn't know how he was doing it. He said he didn't like running long distances and the longest he had ever run was 10K. He looked fresh after 4 hours of running, with not a drip of sweat and no complaints of aching legs. If you saw him, you wouldn't have known he was at the tail end of a 20K run. I was the complete opposite: sweaty, moaning, sore, in pain, and a complete emotional wreck.

There were bends in the road and I couldn't see the finish gantry. I was looking for it intensely, as I was desperate to see it in reality and not just through visualisation. When was this going to end? Where was the finish? With every twist and turn in the road I thought I was going to be able to see it, still nothing. My cousin Paul started to film me on his iPhone as I ran, so I knew I must be close. With no gantry, I focused on some kids on the side of the road, I started to give them a footballer's clap to thank them for their support, then realised it was Ross and Jakob (my son and nephew). The first thing I thought was, those kids are with me, and the second thought was, what the hell were they doing here? In my delusional state I didn't realise how close I actually was to finishing. My daughter Tasha ran toward me, held my hand and ran with me like we did during some of my training runs; it was a great moment seeing the kids. I could not hold on to Tasha's hand long as I was trying to hide my tears by covering my face with my hands.

There it was – after over a year of visualisation, it was right in front of me: the finish gantry. I started what, in my head, was a sprint finish, which just turned out to be my legs saying, 'Thank god it's all most over.' With 50 yards to go, my spirit, mind, and body was overcome with emotion.

Crossing the finishing line, the first person I hugged was a perfect stranger, a guy who probably believed in me more than I did, a guy who had not stopped encouraging me at any point since we'd met, and a guy who became a true legend for me: Rene. The only words

I could muster to say in his ear between bouts of crying was 'Thank you so much.'

My wife, Wendy, put the marathon medal over my head, and as we embraced, she said,

'You did it luv!'

Between the sobs, I replied, 'I know! Can you believe it?'

I think we were both in shock that I had actually finished.

I hugged my kids, I hugged my mum, then my dad, and then pretty much anyone else who wanted a hug. I was an absolute emotional and physical mess, but I didn't care. I had my family around me at the time of an unbelievable achievement in my life; I could not ask for more. I am not sure if anyone could have scripted the last 3 miles; I dare Steven Spielberg to try. At this point, I didn't know if I was coming or going, the gulp crying carried on through the family pictures, and for about 15 minutes after we had all left the finish area.

As my marathon journey ended, I later found out that the motto for the Edmonton marathon was, 'Everyone finishes'. For this, I will be eternally grateful. I may have come last, but everybody involved in this event – the volunteers, the police, the organising committee, the event announcer Mark Connolly, and the staff, made me feel like I came first.

After the hugs, pictures, tears, and laughter, I caught up with Rene to have a quiet word. I told him that what he had done was the most selfless act I had ever seen anybody do for another human being, and I wished I could have given him something for his effort. I wanted to stay in touch. Neither of us had a phone handy, so I wrote my name on a piece of paper and asked him to look me up on Facebook. After more congratulative words from Rene, we had a hardy man hug and went our separate ways. Rene was my running angel on that day and has become a personal hero, and unbeknown to me, it would be many years before we would reconnect.

Every single time I tell my marathon story to anyone who will listen, I get emotional. Even writing it down has brought me back to those last miles and the gulp crying. If you're wondering what my time was for my first and last marathon, it was 07:07:23. I was last, but I wouldn't have wanted it any other way.

I used all my selfies to capture special moments with quotes and words that might inspire others. This was truly a highlight in my life; I had to capture the moment with a momentous quote.

MILE 32

What's the Point?

I didn't take my medal off for at least three days, and the post-run pain was intense. I made a conscious decision to keep walking and even made it to West Edmonton Mall, the largest shopping mall in North America, the very next day. This was an attempt to try and keep the blood flowing and allow the lactic acid to dissipate. In my times of non-movement, I tried to reply to the many notifications I had on all my social networking platforms.

With 'run a marathon' now ticked off my bucket list and all the dust settled, I was now home and back at work. I tried to be humble and only sneaked my marathon run into a few conversations. It took me 15 days to get to the point where I could lace up my shoes and go for a local run without being in pain.

I put on my running garb and crossed the threshold of the doorway like I had done many times before. It was only a short run, but there was a big problem. The image of the finishing gantry was still in my mind's eye. My mind was spinning as I kept experiencing a 'been there, done that, got the t-shirt' moment.

I asked myself, 'What's the point of running now?' Echoes of the doctor's words about diabetes, heart attacks, and strokes were a distant memory; I felt so good. I realised it was the journey towards running a marathon that drove me; without the journey, there was no drive. What was I supposed to do? I was lost.

I was reluctant to do any runs following my marathon experience because runs became a chore; they were no fun and felt like a waste of time. So, I made the decision to stop running. I needed to find something to help me find my running mojo again. Train for another marathon? NO, never again; my marathon run had the most spectacular ending and if I was to run another one, it might taint the memory. If I could be convinced to do another marathon, it would have to be a big one. The only one that I would even think about doing would be The London Marathon. With this in mind, I told myself that I would keep on applying through the entry lottery and deal with my next marathon in the unlikely event that it happened; this left it to fate. I could run another half marathon, but that would be a bit of a damp squib, a step down, and, dare I say, easy. Then I thought about the three half marathons in three weekends I did back in 2015.

From this thought grew the idea of streak goals. This then reminded me of a piece of running trivia that I'd picked up at some point about the running legend Ron Hill. Mr Hill did not miss a day of running between 20th December 1964 and 30th January 2017, a total of 52 years and 39 days. On 20th December 2014, Mr Hill completed Manchester's 5K Heaton Park parkrun, achieving his goal of running at least a mile a day for 50 years. This memory the reminded me about Ben Smith, a 36-year-old from Portishead, Bristol. Ben ran 401 marathons in 401 days. Both streaks were insane and impossible. I was looking for something slightly more achievable to start with.

MILE 33

Streak Running

Like running naked, streak running had nothing to do with showing my wobbly bits. It was all about giving myself a goal, a reason to run, a purpose.

Parkruns were 5K; they took me about 40 to 45 minutes to complete, and I did them most Saturdays. When I wasn't training for something specific, my standard local runs that I did 2 to 3 days a week, were also 5K. I had a fairly easy 5K route already plotted as a loop, starting and ending at my doorstep. Doing some exercise for an hour a day was enough to get my doctor's seal of approval. So, taking all this into account, it was a no brainer; the only question I needed to ask was, could I run 5K every day for two weeks? There was definite potential and I gave it a good think.

On 16th November 2016, only 87 days after my first and last marathon, I started my first running streak challenge.

MILE 34

50.5.50 Challenge

Challenge Criteria: *Run a minimum of 5K or 3.1 miles, every day for 50 days.*

Running 5K every day for two weeks? Why stop at two weeks? Why not a month, six months, or a year? As a happy medium, I decided 50 days in a row would be enough.

This challenge was done under the radar compared to my other race day promotions on social networking, as I didn't really want to set myself up to fail. Timing was going to be the key to getting this challenge done, and finding a work-family-run balance and an hour every day, for the next 50 consecutive days, was going to be the real challenge.

The plan was to wait until the weekend to start the challenge with a parkrun. However, it was only Wednesday, and I had just completed a 4-mile run, so I thought why not start today? I superimposed the run information of the date – 16th November 2017, the distance: 4.05 miles (over 5K), the time: 01:05:01, and 1 of 50, onto a selfie to commemorate the official start of the challenge. I also decided that, from this day forward, for every run, I would take a picture that represented it, add the relevant information to it, and create a finishing poster as a keepsake.

Over the 50 days, the poster became filled with selfies, pictures from parkruns, a 5K race during which everyone was dressed as Santa, artistic pictures, landscape shots, and bleak shots representing appalling runs.

On 3rd January 2017, I finished the challenge. Finding the time seemed easy, but this came down to the support of Wendy who allowed me to take an hour each day to get the miles in, while she took over parenting duties. There were some close calls as there were some runs that were done late at night just before 12:00am, a run that was done when I had a bad flu, and some runs for which I had to wake up at an insane such as 3:30am, just to get them done. The key to this challenge was to think 2, 3, or 4 days ahead, scoping out when I could get the miles in.

It was done, and I felt amazing. I actually thought of keeping the streak alive and continuing. My body said NOPE! Streak challenges were the future and after a few days' rest I had to think of my next challenge.

Challenge started: 16th November 2016

Challenge ended: 3rd January 2017

MILE 35

10.10.10 Challenge

Challenge Criteria: *Run a minimum of 10K, every day for 10 days.*

The next challenge had to take things to a new level to keep me motivated. Only 17 days after finishing the 50.5.50 challenge, I started a new, harder, seemingly impossible task. As my confidence grew with these challenges, so did the exposure of my challenges on my social networking sites. This time, I opened it up to anyone who would be interested in joining me, either in real life or virtually. To be honest, I didn't think I would get anyone to take me up on my offer, but I had a few takers from all over the world, believe it or not; however Rachel Norton-Warsop was the only one who finished this gruelling challenge. She was not only an avid runner but became a supporter of my running journey. We met at a parkrun and became fast friends along with her husband, Si Warsop. Both Rachel and Si had encouraged me to get involved with the running community.

They were both the reason I joined my first running club, Denby Dale Athletics, which was based only six minutes from my house. The group met twice a week: Tuesdays and Thursdays. The distances run on these nights varied, but the overwhelming support was always consistent.

Rachel and I both started the challenge on the same day and most of the time we ran together, virtually. We encouraged each other by writing notes of support when a post-run picture was uploaded to a public Facebook group I'd created. Some days we ran together as Rachel would join me on my local 10K route.

Runs 1, 2 and 3 were doable, runs 3 and 4 were an absolute grind, and runs 5 and 6 were the worst. It was at this point I would have stopped the challenge if Rachel wasn't doing it with me. My body was screaming,

'COME ON SEAN … stop it already!!!'

My mind was saying,

'You are joking!'

Knowing that Rachel had to do, or was doing a 10K that day, drove me to get the miles in.

When Rachel and I met at our weekly running group each Thursday, we didn't have to say anything; we could both see the pain of the challenge on our faces. I was reluctant and embarrassed to mention that I felt like quitting; six 10K runs in a row was extraordinarily tough, let alone doing four more. Even before I got the words out Rachel said,

'I thought of quitting today'

I laughed out loud and said, 'I was just going to say the same thing.'

We were both laughing on the outside, but I am sure, like me, Rachel was crying on the inside; we both knew, in that moment, that we just needed to complete this damn challenge.

Once we got through the tough runs and hit the eighth 10K, the end was in sight. On 29th January 2017, both Rachael and I finished, by far, the most difficult challenge I had ever set myself: 100K in 10 days. This was the toughest thing I'd ever done, next to running a marathon and I needed some proper recovery time. With this being said, while I was soaking in a hot bath of muscle relaxing Epsom salts, I already had my eye on my next running challenge.

Here is the 10.10.10 challenge through Rachel's eyes:

Where do I start? It was a big challenge; the greatest accomplishment and, on reflection, something to be proud of! What has it taught me? The resilience of facing such a challenge is never a lone journey. My first run was entitled 'What has this crazy Canadian gotten me into?' and, for me, it ended with an iconic image of both our hands on the turnaround stone, which was from part of the viaduct, located at the Denby Dale train station; this was symbolic of the trials and tribulations shared over the course of the challenge.

It was January 2017, within a month of the shortest day of the year (21st December), post 'Christmas blowout' and I was feeling sluggish; there wasn`t a great deal of incentive to get out of the door for a run on those bleak early mornings and late nights around 8.30am – 5.00pm work commitments. It was a time of the year I aptly call 'blackout', which means going to work and returning from the work in the dark. I had participated in challenges in the past, namely Jantastic, aimed at maintaining running focus through the limited daylight hours from January to March when the hour 'springs' forward and the world 'brightens up', so to speak. I needed something to keep my foot in the door and prevent me from falling completely off the running map. I knew Sean and his antics from parkrun, not particularly well but enough to be Facebook acquaintances and, living in the locality, I recall he had shown an interest in the running club. When he suggested the challenge, I jumped at the chance, not really thinking about the gravity of the situation. I knew I could run 10K, but could I really run ten 10Ks in ten days? How would I ever accomplish it?

Everyone, whatever their involvement, had an important role in the Challenge. The participants and supporters alike were geographically diverse. As I recall, not all of us were in the 'Endgame' (sorry, I`m a fan); those who didn`t engage in the whole of the Challenge offered valuable support in other ways, even from across the Atlantic Ocean. On a practical level, each participant needed to juggle their own family, work and social commitments, sometimes in different time zones, and the runs were often solitary affairs, for me in the pitch black in sometimes unlit areas. From a safety aspect I wore a head torch, hi-vis jacket and ran with my trusty four-legged friend. More often than not, it was a case of mind over matter and the only thing that kept me going, especially in the first half of the challenge, was the thought of Sean going through the same process and the elation of posting the post-run progress photograph and updating in the Challenge group on social media. The Challenge photo became a highlight of the process for me and it was really quite addictive. It ultimately became a symbol of celebration of the achievement and a shared solidarity, offering a vital insight into how the others were getting along. After a tough run, it lifted the spirits as much as, if not more than, a medal and t-shirt and formed the basis of a fabulous poster at the end of the Challenge.

Overcoming the Challenge wasn`t easy. I had to think of ever more inventive ways of making 100K (62.14 miles to me) in 10 days feel interesting, less monotonous, and more fun. The dark mornings and nights made it practically impossible to do anything other than road run, when my greatest love was the local off-road tracks, paths, and fields. On tired legs, and at a fixed distance, there was no incentive or opportunity to put in a 'fastest' or 'longest' run, so it was all about playing and tinkering with what it was possible to do with 10K. Yes, there were those days that I just ran a steady 10K for sheer enjoyment, although I also incorporated, being geographically blessed, hill miles and elevation challenges into the runs. I was lucky enough to encounter the odd Strava segment along the way and managed some HIIT training and mixed-pace runs, utilising and incorporating warm-ups, loops, lampposts, repeats, and cooldowns. However, by far the best and most memorable days were those on which I had company.

I had the benefit of my four-legged friend, our standard poodle, for company on the solitary runs. After initially missing my usual Tuesday night club run to focus on the Challenge, and regretting it, I made the most of incorporating the Thursday night club run into the challenge, with number 6 entitled 'over the hump – so much easier with the crazy gang'; the club only ran for 4 miles, but I was blessed with Sean`s company to make up the mileage afterwards. I learned early in the challenge that I had made a grave mistake in not utilising my Saturday morning parkrun on day two of the Challenge, ending up running on tired legs later in the day when I felt unwell and thereby needing to take the following day as rest. I wasn't about to make the same mistake on run number 8 when, with the support of my husband, fellow club members and the parkrun family, I incorporated Nostell parkrun. The second 10K of that day, to replace the 'lost run', was the run home from my mother-in-law's house, fuelled by her meat and potato pie. However, the most momentous occasion of all, was during run number 10, when I took the decision to ditch the Meltham 10K in favour of finishing the Challenge with Sean. This was marked by him recording his best time for the Challenge at 01:20:15.

With all the trials and tribulations of the previous nine days devoured, it was an absolute honour on a fine Sunday morning to run with Sean to his half-way marker and capture the perfect end to the Challenge by the 'laying of hands' on his half-way stone. It was a fitting tribute and, for me, symbolic of the hard times shared; the knowledge that each of us faced the same struggles was a driving force and the impetus to put the next foot forward. At the end of 10 days, not only had I run 100K (62.14 miles), but I had also learned a few things about myself. I think the moral of the story is that Sean asked the question and we answered, carried along by his unwavering enthusiasm. The power of the mind is a very strong influence, even when the body is unwilling. Into the bargain, the Challenge was a platform from which I recorded some of my best ever statistics, including the most miles run in one week, one month, and one year. In all, the 10.10.10 Challenge forged strong bonds and set me up for a fabulous 2017. Thank you Sean.' ~ ***Rachel Norton-Warsop***

Rachel and I were both on the verge of giving up, but our determination not to let each other down kept us going. The 10.10.10 was, by far, the toughest streak challenge I set for myself. Huge thanks to Rachel for getting me through it.

Challenge started: 20th January 2017

Challenge ended: 29th January 2017

MILE 36

100.5.100 Challenge

Challenge Criteria: *Run a minimum of 5K every day for 100 days.*

It took me a while to recover from my last challenge; however the time did not go to waste. I was plotting my next challenge in between my routine runs around my local area. This time I was going large, giving people enough notice to join me, and taking my next challenge into the stratosphere.

I learnt a lot about time management, scheduling, and routine during the 50.5.50 challenge. I also learnt a lot about harnessing the support of others during the never-to-be-repeated 10.10.10 challenge. With all this thrown into the mix, the 100.5.100 challenge was born. It was an open challenge to all and the response was surprising; seven people wanted to take the challenge on. Charlotte Hallas, Hayley Stinchon, Jase Windu, Rachel Norton-Warsop, Sam Clee, Shelia O'Carrol, and Si Warsop.

The people attempting this challenge had their own reasons for participating but I was truly honoured they chose to be part of my journey. As a runner who liked running by himself, I was surprised how they embraced me, even with my idiosyncrasies and reluctance to run with others. The group epitomised the positive ethos of the entire running community. The likes, positive comments, well wishes, advice, support, and their friendship truly made me the runner I am today.

As there was more than just me doing this challenge, and it was quite daunting, some formal guidelines had to be put in place to ensure people didn't get overwhelmed, injured, or feel the need to drop out. These rules were agreed by all involved.

Rule #1: A minimum of 5K was to be run each day;

Rule #2: 100 5Ks needed to be run in 100 days; and

Rule #3: If a day was missed, two 5Ks could be run on one day, but a long run could not be split (e.g. one 10K run could not be used as two 5K runs; there had to be recovery time in between)

The rules were to be used as informal guidelines. I was not policing this challenge and would assume that people did the 100 5Ks. My ultimate goal was to get people out running, and if they were doing it safely and enjoying it, I was happy.

If the participants posted a picture that represented their run in the yet another new Facebook group I created, they would get a commemorative poster of their 100 pictures at the end of the challenge. Some people started early, due to scheduling but most started on the same day, Saturday 11th March 2017.

As predicted, the support, banter, advice, thoughts and feelings about the challenge poured out in the form of posts and likes on Facebook. Because it was a public group, posts and likes even came from people who were not participating. Sometimes we would see each other out running as we completed our own routes locally; some days we would make a conscious decision to run together. Some runs were longer than 5K; some runs were official races in some form or another. Even with all these different variables, one thing stayed the same – all the positive vibes –even when we individually hit our respective walls.

I hit my first tiny wall on day 16. On that day, after the run, I posted a picture of me with my head on my pillow with a sad face, which represented how I felt on that day. At the same time, I was asking myself, 'Why the hell did I start this damn challenge?' This feeling was short lived as the overwhelming support from the group and the knowledge that I did 50 runs in a row in the past quickly snapped me out of this funk.

The enthusiasm, drive, and perseverance of the group got me through the dark days of runs 49 to 56. The runs became easier when I got over the hump of 50, but I still couldn't see the light at the end of the tunnel. I will admit there were three days that I just walked the 5K, most days were just 40 to 45 minutes of struggle and there were some that were close to beating my 5K PB.

Run 63 was truly a milestone. It started as a normal run during a fundraising event for a friend of my daughter, Tasha. The event was held at Pugneys Country Park. Pugneys is a family park, which is run by Wakefield Council; it is a 100-acre water sports lake facility used for sailing, wind surfing, canoeing, and kayaking. It also has a 1.6-mile-long running path that surrounds a lake which people walked, rode their bikes, and ran.

On this day, I started my run like any other run, just to get my 5K in for the day. I had run this route a few times before in the past so I knew the lay of the land. I didn't intend to start off fast, but I did, which resulted in just over a 10-minute mile. The weird thing was, I was feeling good and was able to maintain that speed for the second mile. It was not until the start of the 3rd mile that I noticed on my Garmin, I was running at a pace that could match and maybe even beat my personal best of 00:31:59, which I achieved on day 58 of this challenge. I put my head down and drove through the pain in my legs and lungs. I went full throttle, weaving in-between the walkers and prams. I was in full sprint; I was running faster than I had ever run and I took no notice of the funny looks I was getting due to my grunting and groaning. I knew where the 5K finish mark was and I was not stopping until I hit the 3rd lamp post in the car park. As I crossed this imaginary finish line, I pressed the largest button on my Garmin and gasped for air, while I slowed to a walk. I was short of breath, sweating, and really couldn't see straight. I composed myself, found my bearings, caught my breath, and looked at my time with anticipation: 00:29:39! I had broken the 30-minute barrier. I had to look at the distance to make sure it was right: 3.1 miles or 5K on the nose. I was beside myself. There I was, giving it a Tiger Woods fist pump and a loud Ric Flair 'WOOOOO!!'. While parents and grandparents were shielding their kids from this loud, sweaty, tomato-faced freak, I walked back to my car in triumph.

Following this accomplishment, my runs returned to being a drag and a chore, but I never missed a day or a run. It was not until I reached run 75 that I finally started to see the end. The countdown from 25 had started. The pictures were still being posted and I added them to the finished posters every five days or so. It was exciting as the last run got closer and closer. For the final run, we decided to run it together.

The 100th run on 19th June became a bit of an event with friends and family meeting at The Dunkirk Pub in Denby Dale. Signs were made, balloons were given out, and family members became cheerleaders. The final run became more of a reflective stroll down memory lane; we shared our thoughts and feelings about the challenge and our individual highs and lows. It was great hearing people's stories and how they thought they would never be able to do it, but did.

A week later, the commemorative posters were finished, printed, and put in frames. Delivering them gave me a chance to catch up on a one-to-one basis to really hear people's introspective thoughts. It was a privilege to hear what they thought of the challenge and the reasons they chose to participate.

Hayley Stinchon was one of the first to join the challenge.

'The sun was shining and I picked myself up after yet another few days of living in a migraine hangover and set off for a walk with the dog. I bumped into Sean and commended him on his running. I mentioned how I was amazed at his discipline and how I wished I had such willpower. That's when he said the sentence that would map out my next 12 months in the most positive way, 'I'm considering running 5K every day for 100 days, why don't you join me?' At first, I laughed, then came to the conclusion he was clearly mad, and that was that.

Then, something snapped inside my brain and, after an hour or two, I found him on Facebook and private messaged him. I wanted in. I wanted to get my health back. I needed a focus. I roped in my old C25K mate, Charlotte, and asked her to join me. Her initial reaction was the same as mine, but my magical persuasive powers changed her mind. I met with Charlotte a few days later and we agreed that we would give it a go. We wouldn't get hung up on the 100 days and would just take each day as it comes. In all honesty I thought I would be happy enough if I even got to 20 days.

We had a few runs with Sean, sometimes we went out separately, sometimes I went speed walking with mum and Charlotte and I joined a running club at which we made some amazing friends. I always had the support of someone and the dog had the time of her life!

My biggest concern was my migraines; once one hits, I'm out of the game for at least 12 hours and then spend the next 24–36hrs in a world of fog and exhaustion. I wasn't free from migraines during this 100-day period but if I had to miss a day, I would make up for it the following day or the day after. I didn't run every 5K either, some were walked. This frustrated me at times, but as time went on, I absolutely loved my walks, it was a time to have a good gossip with my mum and catch up on life.

When I hit day 50, I was over the moon; I'd far surpassed my goal and felt stronger than ever. By day 75 I was really feeling the exhaustion, but that elusive 100 wasn't far away and there was no way I would be giving up now. The running club was my absolute rock – we got together at least once a week and as there were members from the club attempting the same challenge, we kept each other going.

Day 100 came around and I was overwhelmed with emotion. It was a Sunday and most of the challenge runners came along to support me and Charlotte in our last run, as well as our families. I was so proud of myself and I felt amazing.

I want to say a massive thank you to everyone who joined me on my challenge, in particular my mum as she would happily get up at 5am to fit in a lovely walk before work and take in many sunrises with me. Sean, simply thank you; thank you for giving me that kick up the backside when I needed it most – oh and an even bigger thank you for the amazing photo collage of every single 5K I completed to remind me of that wonderful time in my life. 100.5.100, you will never be forgotten.' ~ ***Hayley Stinchon***

***

Sheila O'Carroll was another runner I had met on my running journey. Sheila not only became one of my running heroes; she also became one of my biggest and best supporters. When I sent out the invite for the challenge via Facebook, her reply felt like a reluctant yes.

'I didn't know Sean from Adam, apart from seeing (and hearing!) him at a couple of our training sessions. He'd been invited to join in a couple of sessions of hill training to see if he thought joining a club would help him achieve his fitness goal, so he came along.

I just loved his absolute vocal honesty about how tough one of the sessions was, at a particularly hilly park that tested legs and lungs to the limit. I struggled too but tried to smile my way round. I'd joined the running club in the hope of improving my practically non-existent fitness level. My gut feeling was that we wouldn't be seeing much of Sean again. How wrong was I and how little did I know of this man's absolute determination despite his struggles!?

I saw little of Sean for a while, but I followed his progress on social media and couldn't help but admire his dogged determination to complete the challenges he set himself. One of these was the 100.5.100 challenge.

Scrolling through my newsfeed one morning with my feet up, drinking coffee, and enjoying the chocolate biscuits I was indulging in, I briefly saw Sean's post about his 100.5.100 challenge and just scrolled on. When the last biscuit went down and I'd almost finished my coffee, curiosity got the better of me and I scrolled back to take a closer look at what Sean was on about now!

A challenge of running / jogging / walking 5K every day for 100 days.

He was asking if anyone would like to join him in his challenge and set up a 100.5.100 group. The immediate thoughts for me were: a) he's barmy; and b) no way could I do that. I didn't doubt Sean's motivation but I certainly doubted mine! I got up and carried on with my day.

Over the following few days, Sean's crazy challenge kept tapping me on the shoulder saying, 'Why don't you try it? 'You don't have to finish it, it's all about the trying bit'. The voice on my other shoulder was knocking me back with things like 'Nah, you're too old; you can't commit; you might injure yourself; it's too much for you, Sheila'.

But still, it nagged at me. I asked a couple of friends their opinions. Of course they said, 'Yeah, give it a go. You can do that! 5K is very doable!' In hindsight, it's funny that none of them did it with me. It was very definitely a challenge but I was beginning to see where Sean got his motivation from. The voice tapping my shoulder kept at me: 'Do it Sheila! Do it!'

The great organiser that he is, Sean had a plan. He set up daily entries/ photographs on a page to create a framed collage of the 100 days. That was my carrot for joining Sean in his challenge of the 100 5Ks in 100 days! The date for the grand start was finalised; all we had to do was make that start and carry on from there.

Day 1 started on parkrun day with plenty of folk willing to smile for a pic with me on that one; and so it went on, rain, hail, or snow, we were out there. There were days when it was an absolute joy to be out there greeting the day, watching the season develop into its natural beauty, and there were the days when it was absolute torture and it would take plenty of self-talk to even get the trainers on!

I'd never in my 60+ years given myself a task to stick to for so long! I gradually began to understand the mindset of those lone marathon and ultra-marathon people (not that I would ever be in that league, but I could see Sean up there with the rest of them).

I learnt to change my thinking from negativity to positivity by ticking off those daily achievements and giving myself permission to pat myself on the back. The more days I got behind me, the fitter I became. The joy and laughter we all had comparing our daily blogs, which provided a sense of comradeship and unity; we were trudging this road together!

On day 50, we got together to celebrate and had a sneak peek of the individual posters that Sean was preparing for us. As a happy coincidence, halfway through this challenge, I ran my 50th parkrun!

All we had to do was write a few words about the 5K that day, take a pic and submit it to the Facebook page. Sean was not only doing his 5K every day, he was the guy doing the background work, making this thing come alive and real!

How could I stop now? Even though way back, I thought I'd call it a day at 50 and be content with that, NO WAY was I stopping halfway through! The 500K mileage and the sense of achievement was too much to let go of. The Show Must Go On! And so, it did.

That final 100th day came. A day to celebrate: balloons, posters, cheers, sunshine, family, friends – what a gathering! Plenty ran with us, for fun and pure joy of finishing this crazy endeavour that, in the end, turned out to be one of the proudest moments of my life. All down to one man and his ambitions and dreams, Sean.

Sean gave us all permission to believe in ourselves and make that dream a reality. Without him, I, for one, would've missed the sheer joy and elation of achieving what I thought was, for me, impossible. Sean, you've taught me the truth behind the saying, never say never.' ~ ***Sheila O'Carroll***

***

If there is one thing that I learnt about myself on the completion of this challenge is that I cannot use the excuse, 'I don't have time'. For 100 days I found at least an hour a day to do something I wanted to do – something I needed to do. I realised that if you have the motivation, purpose, drive, and support, you will make time. Who would have thought it, I taught myself a life lesson that I still use today. The next question was; what was my next challenge going to be?

It took me a few months to recover after the 100.5.100 challenge. I still did intermittent runs, entered a few official races but ran without a major goal, which, once again became a bit of a drag. What could I possibly do that would really test my limits? 5Ks? 10Ks? Been there – done that. Then it hit me, the original progression of my running was 5K, then 10K, then the Great North Run. At the time, half marathons became the inevitable evolution of my running journey. I did three half marathons in three consecutive weeks; how could I possibly top that streak? Hmmmm.

Challenge started: 11th March 2017

Challenge ended: 19th June 2017

Left to right: Sean Kachmarski, Sheila O'Carroll, Jase Windu. I awarded the group's hard work with a ceremonial framed keepsake. 100 selfies – each selfie represented our thoughts or feelings about each run we completed.

This was my keepsake for the 100.5.100 Challenge. If you look closely, you will see the time in which I ran the 5K, the date, and some words that summed up the run. The dotted boxed pictures were 5K highlights, such as the day I broke the 30-minute barrier or other PBs. My current 5K PB is 00:29:39, #63 of 100.

MILE 37

Three Half Marathons in Three Days Challenge

Challenge Criteria: *Run three half marathons on three consecutive days.*

Was this even possible? Recovery between races was not my strong suit and back-to-back-to-back half marathons left literally no time for recovery. I really needed to think about this one as I didn't want to set myself up to fail, or worse, hurt myself.

Not thinking anyone would want to, as this was a bonkers challenge, I had to ask myself the question, 'Should I post the challenge on Facebook and see if there were other foolish people interested?' Well I did – and there was. Enter Leyla Brooke.

I can't remember the first time I officially met Leyla. In the early days of my running career, I just knew of her, and, if I was honest, I was in awe of her. Leyla is a proper runner: 5K, 10K, half marathons, marathons, ultra-marathons and even though she had travelled the world to participate in high-profile races she was grounded, down to earth, and humble – a true inspiration. Having Leyla joining me on this challenge, in my eyes, it was like having Paula Radcliffe on board.

'To be honest, I can't remember how I met Sean, but I can remember watching his challenges from afar and thinking 'wow', seeing how inspirational he is. I think Sean's determination is amazing. I admire how he constantly wants to push the boundaries to see how far he can go and what he can achieve. I believe you can achieve anything you put your mind to.' ~ ***Leyla Brooke***

I started this challenge on 1st September 2017, 74 days after the 100.5.100 challenge. Plus, I needed it to be a long weekend so I booked the Monday off work to get it done. The date was set, the route was calculated, and the challenge was splashed all over social media; there was no turning back (especially when you have the most iconic runner you know agreeing to do it with you).

The earlier in the day the better, was my strategy for the first of three. My thought process was, if I get it out of the way early in the day, I could have my hot bath, endure a foam roller session and be recovered for the second 13.1-miles in less than 24 hours. This meant a 5:00am start on a Saturday, which was actually a nice start to the day. The route I had planned was an out and back, finishing with the original 5K loop that I had used many times in other challenges.

Dare I say the first was easy? Upon reflection, there was a combination of things that made it comfortable: I knew the route so well that I could gauge how far I needed to go without looking at the GPS watch; there were no hills per se, but the 1st half had an almost unnoticeable incline that I was able to endure; ultimately, what made it easy was at the turnaround point, the unnoticeable incline became a very noticeable decline. I finished the first half marathon in 03:00:29, a respectable time for me, but I figured that this challenge was more about the ability to recover, than the actual miles or time.

Soaking in the hot bath following the first run, my mind was at ease as my legs were aching and sore, but not as bad as I thought they would be. Plop went the isotonic tablet into a cool glass of water; a few bananas disappeared into my NutraBullet as I blended a protein shake; and the foam roller sat in the corner of the room as if to say, 'Let's Roll!'

My body and legs were sore and tight but I could walk up and down stairs without wincing. I had planned to do the next run in the afternoon of the following day, so my thought process was, with an early bedtime, my body would recover ready for the next run.

Much to my amazement, it worked! In the morning I was wanting to get it done, so I did. Not waiting for my pre-determined start time of later in the day, I was out the door to do my second half marathon in less than 24 hours. Dare I say it was easy? No! It was shite! It was a grind – a slow grind around my local half marathon route, again. It was brutal. I was so eager to get out of the door, I wasn't prepared; I forgot my gels; I also had to stop at the local Co-Op for a Lucozade and probably walked 30% of the distance. A crap run in my books. I should have stuck to my start times I had carefully thought through. Much to my surprise, my time was only 9 minutes slower than the previous day: 03:09:22.

After this run, I was ready to throw in the towel. Two half marathons in less than 24 hours was enough. But, looking at my social networking sites, I knew I had to find one more within me from somewhere. Plop went the isotonic tablet into a cool glass of water … again. Three bananas disappeared into my NutraBullet as I blended a protein shake … again. This time I gave two fingers to the foam roller sat in the corner of the room. It was time for a hot soak and an early night … again.

The next day, I did NOT want to get up. I was in pain. I tried to talk myself out of running that day,

'If I run this next one, I may injure myself.'

'Two half marathons in less than 24 hours is enough!'

'Who the hell set this challenge anyway? What an ASSHOLE!'

Then my mindset flipped;

'Only one more to go!'

'I don't want to post that I didn't get it done.'

'It's called a challenge for a reason.'

Looking at Leyla's post-run messages and words of encouragement on Facebook, inspired me. I knew a half marathon run was basically a warmup distance for her, so I knew she would nail the challenge. It would be commonplace for me to see her run a 20-mile or 25-mile session on Strava. At the end of the day, Leyla took time out of her day away from her family to do my silly challenge; how could I let her down?

Even with all this motivation, I still struggled, so the question was: 'How could I get out of the door to get the third run done?' There was only one way I was going to get out of the door, but it was a bit of a risk. Asking anyone on Facebook if they wanted to run my last half marathon with me, was the only way for me to get out of that door. It would literally take another runner grabbing me by the scruff of the neck and dragging me out. The risk was who, and how many would actually reply at such short notice? Surely none … I secretly hoped.

I posted an invite to join me via Facebook, and within 30 seconds my plan backfired. Leyla posted a comment, 'I'm in, what time?' Within another minute, another runner, Rick Green, posted a comment under Leyla's, 'When are you planning to run?' CRAP, I was now committed and had to run my final half marathon with two of the fastest runners

I know. I really didn't think this strategy through, but it worked. I was out of the door as Leyla and Rick showed up for my final run.

Running with others as I've previously mentioned, was always something I struggled with, but running with people who were clearly faster and were used to a much quicker pace was a waking nightmare. I took a risk in asking and I now had to live with the consequences. When running with faster and stronger runners, I always have this overwhelming sense that I am holding them back. Running a 3-hour half marathon when you are used to running a half marathon in 90 minutes must be frustrating.

In the end, I did see it as a privilege to run with two well-established runners. They both reassured me by saying if they didn't want to run with me, they would not have accepted my invite. I thanked them again for joining me and we were on our way.

The three of us chatted all the way around, about the past, the present, and the future. The discussions were deep, fun, serious, and heartfelt, which took my mind off the pain I was in. With all the chit-chat, the run was over before I knew it. Weirdly, it turned out to be the fastest time of the three days, 03:00:29.

So, I had done it again; another challenge was finished. I once again, achieved the impossible, with the unwavering support of my friends. It was now time to re-enter the running limbo.

Challenge Started: 1st September 2017

Challenge Ended: 3rd September 2017

So, what's next? I didn't know. I not only entered running limbo, but a shame spiral. I needed a challenge to motivate me; with no motivation I was not running and with no running, my moods swings were extreme – just ask Wendy. I failed to get an entry into the 2018 London Marathon, so I had to think outside the box.

Revisit a past challenge? No. Extend a streak past 100? No. Instead of distances go for speed and PBs? No. I then thought about the toughest streak to date, the 10.10.10 challenge. Could I do 20, 30, 50 10Ks consecutively? Definitely NO! I would need some sort of break in between runs, but then it would not be a streak, I declared to myself. It took me a while – three months in fact – to discover what was staring me in the face.

Left to right: Sean Kachmarski, Rick Green, Leyla Brooke. I asked the two fastest runners I know to run the third half marathon of three in a row with me. What the hell

MILE 38

100.10.1 Challenge

Challenge Criteria: *Run 100 10Ks in 1 year*

On New Year's Day, 2018, I started the 100.10.1 challenge; this is the first selfie for yet another commemorative framed keepsake.

I thought of this challenge at the beginning of December 2017 and was chomping at the bit to get started. I had an entire month to get my head around it as I set the start date as 1st January 2018. A new year and a new year-long challenge; 52 weeks to run 100 10Ks? That worked out at 1.92 runs per week. Easy right? Well … let's see.

The month-long wait gave me time to recruit suckers … I mean people who might want to attempt this challenge with me. A commemorative framed photo of the accomplishment was, once again, used as incentive during my pitch. This approach worked like a charm; I got four willing participants to take part: Jase Windu, a runner who I met at parkrun and was a big supporter; Julia Church, a person I met via Facebook who was a friend of Briony Bullard and lived in Australia; Rachel Norton-Warsop, a 100.5.100 and 10.10.10 challenge participant; and, of course, the legend – Leyla Brooke.

We all started on the same day – 1st January 2018. We posted our selfies in the new Facebook group I'd created and we were all determined to get this done. Having the challenge to focus on allowed me to get my running mojo back. Some weeks I would do three or four 10Ks; other weeks, I would do none. My average 10K took me 01:23:45. So from going out the door, doing the run, getting in and out of the shower, and then to the couch was a two-hour chunk out of my day. Having the rest days were a godsend when my legs, body, mind, and heart screamed 'NOT TODAY!' The hardest part of this challenge was that every run had to be 10K. I missed the basic head-clearing turbo 2- or 3-mile runs. I could have done them, but I saw them as a waste of energy and time. If I was out the door for a run, it was going to be a 10K.

For the most part, it was a good challenge; it got me out the door at least two days a week and with work, family, and life in general, the weeks of the year seemed to pass faster than usual. Was it because I was counting the number of weeks left in the year in relation to the number of runs left? I'm not sure, but there were times that I thought

I might have to start doubling up on the runs to get them in before the end of the year. Thankfully, I didn't have to.

However, during the year, I did enter some official races:

Run 18: 2018 Oulton Park 10K (01:11:52)
Run 23: 2018 Wakefield 10K (01:12:44)
Run 50: 2018 Leeds 10K (01:19:30)
Run 70: 2018 Shepley 10K (01:22:00)
Run 75: 2018 Sheffield 10K (01:17:10)

Of these official races, the most noteworthy was my 70th 10K of the year, the 2018 Shepley 10K. It was a local race about 10 minutes from my house and there was nothing particularly special about the race itself; it was more about who I ran it with and what we discussed as we ran.

As Leyla was doing the 100.10.1 challenge with me, she always told me of local 10K races I might be interested in. The Shepley 10K was one of those races and she agreed to slum it and run it with me. I am not sure if it was a part of her evil master plan, but after this race, Leyla planted the seed for my next challenge … and it was BEYOND ridiculous.

Let me just take a step back and tell you why I am in such awe of Leyla. Leyla has run in the London, Berlin, and Chicago Marathons. She has registered for the 2019 New York Marathon and has her sights set on the Tokyo and Boston Marathons. Leyla participated in three of my past challenges and while doing this challenge, she simultaneously did a 12 marathons in 12 months challenge, and three of them were ultras. Leyla is a genuine celebrity to me when it comes to running. What also amazes me about her is the fact that she has a job, three kids, and a husband – what an absolute icon.

During what felt like a routine Shepley 10K, the topic of my next challenge came up. I bounced some ideas off Leyla and told her that I had my sights on running the London Marathon as my next challenge.

I did admit to her that at the end of the 2016 Edmonton Marathon, I had emphatically screamed NEVER AGAIN! However, with time, the pain was forgotten and the idea of doing another marathon tiptoed back into my consciousness. It took me three years to consider putting myself through that pain again. I discussed leaving it to fate and just applying through the London Marathon entry lottery, knowing that only 6% get in that way. I also contemplated raising money to get a charity spot. Even though it was for a good cause and good karma, I would not only have to pay £100 to enter, but also raise between £1,500 and £2,500, depending on which charity I selected. Trying to deal with a work-family-training-AND-fundraising balance might be a bit too much. Ultimately, I never liked asking people for money, so I was conflicted. After about 2 miles of me doing all the talking and trying to justify and explain the pros and cons of having the London marathon as my next challenge. Leyla just said,

'Why do you want to run another marathon?'

'Ummm … because it's the London Marathon; it's local and it's kind of iconic.' I said triumphantly, trying to convince myself more than Leyla.

'It's still only 26.2 miles. You've already done that. You've already ticked "run a Marathon" off your bucket list', said Leyla, grinning mischievously.

Leyla knew she had me right where she wanted me; she knew she now had my attention. I do concede that, at that moment, Leyla peaked my interest.

'I guess you're right – what should my next challenge be then?' I asked, sheepishly. I kind of knew what her answer was going to be and I couldn't believe I was even going to consider the next three words that came out of her mouth.

'An ultra-marathon', she said.

Amazingly, my initial reaction was not 'NO CHANCE! ARE YOU CRAZY!??'

It was, 'How far is an ultra?'

'An ultra is any distance over a marathon distance, usually 50K or 50 miles to start', Leyla explained, gingerly as if she knew she had me on the hook and was slowly reeling me in. She then went in for the kill by adding the following statement:

'A 50K race is only 4.8 miles more than a marathon – you can handle that. You can then call yourself an ultra-runner.'

It was at this point that the word 'ultra' was added to my running vocabulary, in much the same way as the word 'marathon' was added after a conversation with John May over four years ago.

I didn't reply at first. I just let those words hangout there for a minute. The words 'only 4.8 miles more to become an ultra-runner' entered my ears and settled in my brain. Consciously and subconsciously, the seed had been planted. Just like with an earworm, I could not shake off the thought that my next challenge was going to be an ultra.

By this time, it was the last mile of the Shepley 10K and it was downhill so there was no time to continue the conversation. It was time for the famous Kachmarski sprint finish. I finished the Shepley 10K in 01:22:00.

The final 29 runs turned out to be a bit of a grind as nothing out of the ordinary happened. Number 100 was held on 10th October, so this challenge would end on the 10th month on the 10th day, which I thought was kind of poetic. For this final run, I would be joined by Leyla and another true running friend, Tracy Hughes. Both volunteered to pace me, because for my last run, I was going for speed. My current overall 10K PB was out of reach as it was run on a very flat 2017 Wakefield 10K road race, and my local route was very hilly.

I just gunned it on this final run as Tracy set the pace in front, while Leyla trailed to ensure I didn't stop or slow down. I ran at times when I usually walked, I sprinted when I usually ran. It was a non-stop, heart pumping, lung busting run that brought back tomato face from the early years. I broke every Strava segment achievement with a finish time of 01:15:38, a new local route PB. I was chuffed; I was sore; I was out of breath; and, more importantly, I had completed another challenge that I had set for myself.

Yes, during the 100.10.1 challenge, Leyla planted the seed for me to do an ultra-marathon. It was during the local Shepley 10K in 2018. Also known as number 70 of 100 in the challenge.

We were now done; the final selfies were taken, and the commemorative frames were created and distributed. I took a week off running to recover, but I also used the time to think of a way to tell my wife about my next challenge. Training for a marathon put her through an emotional ringer, and I didn't know how she was going to react when I told her that I'd secretly signed up for a 50K ultra.

Leyla Brooke, with her own 100.10.1 commemorative keepsake for her own wall of fame.

On the 10th day of the 10th month in 2018, I had finished 100 10Ks in 1 year. The finish date seemed ironic.

MILE 39

What Have I Done!?

Confession time; the night following the Shepley 10K, I was awake for hours. Not basking in the glory of a well-run race; I was secretly in search of an ultra. It was tougher than I thought as I had very specific criteria:

- No finishing time limit set
- Flat
- No trail running
- Local
- Many, many runners

I soon realised that most ultras were on trails, which sucked, and due to the nicheness of ultra-running, the entry numbers were always low, which doubled sucked. I was not discouraged, with the 'only 4.8 miles more to become an ultra-runner' assertion still ringing in my ears, I spent at least three hours looking for the best ultra for me. I message Leyla several times, 'What about this one?' 'Have you run this one?' 'Do you think this one would be ok?' Leyla was the only person who knew I was considering and actively looking for a race and these late-night texts made it feel like I was doing something nefarious.

Then I found one; the Canal Canter Summer Extravaganza Ultra ticked most of my boxes. It was flat, local, out and back, and 50K, only 4.8 miles more than a marathon.

The 2019 Canal Canter Summer Extravaganza Ultra description, via the website:

'As the name suggests, this is an out and back canter on the Leeds and Liverpool Canal. The route will start and finish at Kirkstall about 2.5 miles outside the centre of Leeds. Whilst this flat route is not particularly technical, it's a great opportunity to improve your own PB. The Leeds and Liverpool Canal is 127.25 miles in length, stretching between the busy cities of Leeds and Liverpool. It is, in fact, the longest canal in the north of England, passing through 91 locks. Its construction began in 1770 and was completed in 1816. For those who are interested, the engineers were John Longbottom, James Brindley, and Robert Whitworth. Foulridge Tunnel, which is part of the Leeds and Liverpool canal, has some interesting folklore surrounding it. The story goes that a cow fell into the water at one end of the tunnel; the cow then swam the whole length of the tunnel, (1 mile) before being pulled out at the other end and thankfully revived with Brandy. So … don't get any ideas; no brandy will be available to revive any desperate runners. "Eeh bah gum, dunt fall int cut, as we waint be cumin in after thee"'

The race was on 15th June 2019, which gave me more than 30 weeks to train and, as a bonus, Leyla said she would run it with me. All the planets were aligning again, so with a few clicks of the mouse and the 16 digits from my credit card, I entered a 50K ultra.

After reading the confirmation email that landed in my email box, I felt a wave of fear and asked myself, 'What the hell have I done?' As my finish to the Edmonton marathon was so epic, I honestly felt nothing was going to top that feeling or experience. Should I have just let sleeping dogs lie? Should I have not tempted fate by opening the door to failure? Only time would tell and my focus now turned to making sure that I did not let my family, friends, Leyla, or myself, down.

MILE 40

Unfinished Business

I have been very fortunate in my life; career wise, I always seemed to land on my feet. In the 20+ years before working for Leeds City Council, I would not only change jobs, but consistently change my career every two years. I had been a youth director with the YMCA in Calgary, a Tournament Events Manager with Alberta Golf, a Recreation Specialist with Royal Caribbean, which evolved into being an Assistant Cruise Director. I was a tutor at the New Zealand Institute of Sport, then back to an Assistant Cruise Director position with Princess Cruise Lines, an Event Manager for the 2005 and 2008 Leeds Half Marathon, a Volunteer Coordinator with Age Concern, Sheffield, followed by a nine-year stint with Leeds City Council as a Training and Development Officer, which ended due to the absolute incompetence of the senior leadership team which left a bad taste in my mouth.

Intertangled in my life-long career pathway there was a failed marriage in Canada, a failed attempt to migrate the family back to Canada from the UK, and work with a so-called well-being company that, ironically, almost killed me, through stress. As I said earlier, the details might, in fact, be another riveting page turner one day.

With all that behind me, I found a job that enabled me to use every tool in my professional toolbox and all the resources I had accumulated throughout my ever-changing career. Public speaking, coordination, building connections, motivating, inspiring, and in my eyes, truly making a difference and having a positive impact as a personal development and wellbeing trainer for a small fast-turnaround printing company. The minute I walked in for my interview. it felt like home.

The Bluetree Group is an established and rapidly expanding retailer and manufacturer of prints and proudly sports the title of Sunday Times Virgin Fast Track 100. The company operates several brands tailored to different print buyers, from end consumers to print resellers. It caters for micro and small businesses right up to multinational FTSE100 companies and invests in its people as much as it does in technology to stay committed to its innovation promise; in 2017, the company created more than 60 jobs and invested £5m in new technology. In addition, it never uses printing presses older than four years to make sure that it delivers a top quality and fast service using the best techniques to people all over the world.

When I started, the company only had 300 staff who were divided between office staff and production staff; it was my job to motivate, inspire, educate, and support the staff in a variety of areas such as well-being, sleep, change management, leadership communication, and health and safety, to name a few. The atmosphere had a high-energy, work hard, play hard feel to it. It felt like I was surrounded by millennials but there were some staff about the same age as me, who could still show the young bucks a thing or two. It was like a fountain of youth when I came to work, as they all seemed to embrace my training style and way of working. In the first three months of being there, the company employed more than 350 people and I started doing something that I never enjoyed doing professionally before: spending time with colleagues outside of work.

The first thing I did was combine my work with the young and energetic folk with my training for the ultra, which meant fun relay events. I Googled 'local relay running events'. What came up almost made me gip – the 2019 Manchester Marathon. Seeing those words prompted a flash back to my failed attempt. The only thing that stopped me from scrolling past quickly was the word 'relay'.

What caught my attention was the tag line:

'Manchester Marathon Relay: Take on the distance in a team of 2 or 4! If 26.2 miles sounds a little too daunting, why not team up with friends, family, or colleagues to cover the distance between you?'

Teams of four sounded interesting with just over 6 miles each – easy.

I quickly wrote out an email with most of the details, inviting anyone who wanted to join the team I was getting together; the subject line read 'Runners Assemble'. I bcc'd the entire company at 9:07 am.

9:08am 'I'm in' from Craig Quinn.

9:10am 'I'm in' from Andrew Moore.

9:11am 'Great! Where do I sign up?' from Charlotte Appleton.

9:15am 'What a great idea! I'm in!' from Deni Stanley.

The emails kept coming and, in total, 15 people were interested. Being new I didn't want to exclude anyone from this opportunity, so I had to explain that although I only needed three runners for my team, others could make their own teams from those who were interested. I also knew that people saying they were interested and actually paying the entry fee were two different things, so I told them that I'd paid the combined entry fee and the first people to pay me back would be on my team.

At 9:45am, my PayPal account burst into action with three people (Craig Quinn, Andrew Moore, and Charlotte Appleton) paying for their entry into the 2019 Manchester Marathon Relay event on 7th April. In the end, we had three teams of four runners from the Bluetree Group organised to run in the event. I supported the captains from the other teams to ensure they didn't lose motivation to train or a willingness to participate.

During our first team meeting, we talked about who was going to do which leg of the race. These three did not know of my disastrous finish of the 2016 Manchester Marathon; the real reason I wanted to do this race was to run the 4th leg and symbolically finish this damn race. I didn't know how to explain this to them without them getting bored with my story, so I said nothing and we decided to draw numbers. Four pieces of paper with 1 through to 4 written on them were folded and put into a hat. Charlotte picked first – 2, so she was to run the second leg. Craig picked next –1, so he was going to start us off. I now had a 50/50 chance of being able to finish the Marathon route. Andrew was next; I closed my eyes, held my breath and willed the next number to be a 3. He picked the folded piece of paper out of the hat, then got distracted by a phone call. As Andrew picked up the phone he threw the paper down; it was the number 3. I let out an audible sigh of relief as this meant that I was 4th and was finally going to be able to finish the marathon in the city in which I'd had so much bad luck. Fate won, yet again.

I continued my usual local training and, at work, the morale in the office was growing due to the relay banter between the three teams. Before I knew it, the day had arrived. The atmosphere of race day was electric, as usual. However, the excitement reached a fevered pitch as the three teams met at a pre-arranged meeting point and the banter, common purpose, and anticipation grew. I was determined to finish this damn marathon, but as an added bonus, the team building element of the relay really overshadowed this moment of closure. Even before the race started, there were laughs, tears, high fives and hugs between me and my co-workers, which was unfamiliar to me, but weirdly soothing.

Mingling with co-workers outside of work is something that I'd never done; there had always been a 'work' Sean and a 'non-work' Sean. I always felt that if the two Seans were to meet, something catastrophic would happen. As I was enjoying the moment with my colleagues, there was no sign of a rip in the space time continuum, ending the world as I knew it. This was something that I needed to continue in the future, because, with this company, it just felt right.

We walked the first leg runners to the start line, then started our own journey to our preselected relay points. As there were three teams, Tim, Jacob, and I hopped on the train to get to our change-over point. Knowing we had at least a two and a half hour wait, we took it slowly. Not admitting we got lost a few times, we eventually made it to the school gym that had been turned into a makeshift runner's exchange point, with plenty of time to waste.

Not knowing when we needed to be ready, we could only use the guesstimated times the three runners said they could run their distance in, so it was a bit of a long shot. On paper, Tim's team was the fastest so we got him ready. Jacob and I waited at the changeover point anticipating that the next person was Tim's relay partner. Thirty minutes later, the change happened and Tim was off, replaced by a heavy breathing and sweaty Johnathan.

Jacob and I didn't know who would be next so we just had to wait with bated breath. During the wait, I experienced every runner's nightmare. For lack of a better phrase I needed a bowel movement, CRAP! No pun intended. I just knew that if I went, Andy, the runner of leg three on my team, would show up; if I waited, well ... it could get messy. So, I dashed and flushed to only return and wait. Then it happened; Andy ran around the corner but, with all my waiting, I was still in shock! I still had my jacket on and I needed to get my earphones in and other bric-a-brac on. Let's just say it was no Formula 1 change over or pit stop. With just a 'well done' shouted in the direction of Andy, I was off.

The first thing that I noticed leaving the relay area, was the speed I was going. It was my usual pace at the start of any race, but there was a contrast in my pace and everybody else's. I was passing people; my fresh legs propelled me past the people who, in my eyes, were the 'real' runners. For clarity, to me, 'real' runners are runners who finish marathons in 2, 3, or 4 hours; the ones who never walk, not ever. As I passed people, even with my headphones in, I could hear runners commenting as I passed,

'What the hell? Oh, it's a relay runner!'

Then somebody would pass me, and I would find myself saying,

'What the hell? Oh, it's a relay runner.' Followed by an internal monologue of,

'I'm slowing down, damn! I started off too fast … again!'

I eventually settled into my usual pace and the non-relay people were now passing me. I didn't mind; the only thing on my mind was, 'I was going to finish this damn thing.' Then it struck me, I was approaching the area where I was stopped those three years ago; The Premier Inn on the right and the wall I sat on watching a fox and a chicken arguing with the marshal. I was now approaching the bend that I never reached the first time around. I had fresh legs with 6 miles to go in a marathon; this was epic!

The actual miles made this just another run. However, as I passed people who were clearly struggling, my mind returned to the Edmonton Marathon and Rene. I thought to myself, should I stop and help these people get across the finish line? To return the favour to a perfect stranger, I did stop to see how some people were doing, gave them some water, gave them some words of encouragement and tried to be their Rene. They weren't having any of it and just waved me on. Some said thanks, others didn't speak, some I felt were fighting their own demons as they hit their wall. I just carried on, knowing I was going to finish.

As I approach a finish gantry, I usually turn on the jets for my famous sprint finish. The issue with this run was that I could see the finish gantry and it seemed to be half a mile away; it was a long straight finish. I was used to a finish of 100, 200, maybe 300 yards. This finishing stretch caused me to run at least three separate sprint attempts. I would turn on the jets, realise it was too far away to maintain that speed and slow down only to start another sprint and slow down again. By the time I could actually do a sprint finish I was way too tired. So, my crossing of the finish line was a bit anticlimactic, speed wise.

Leg 1: 5.32 miles (00:43:13) Craig Quinn

Leg 2: 5.57 miles (01:22:28) Charlotte Appleton

Leg 3: 8.34 miles (01:15:37) Andrew Moore

Leg 4: 6.98 miles (01:28:48) Sean Kachmarski

Total Time: 04:50:06

As I crossed the finish line, I imagined finishing the 2016 Manchester Marathon, falling into the arms of my wife and kids and, of course, my mum. However, this time my legs felt fresh and there was an actual crowd of people,

'So, this is what it feels like to finish a marathon quickly', I thought to myself.

As I got the coveted marathon medal placed around my neck, I slammed the book closed on this damn race and looked for my team.

The ironic end to this story was, even though the rest of my team got a medal the same as mine, their straps read 'Marathon Relay' and mine just said 'Marathon'. This was great; I could now tell my grandchildren many years from now that I ran the entire 2019 Manchester marathon and leave out the bit about it only being a relay. **#Closure**

MILE 41

An Ultra. Really?

Truth? My head was not 100% into doing an ultra like it was when I focused on my marathon. An ultra was so far out of my comprehension that doubt washed over me every time I thought about actually running the 50K. It was over 23 weeks away and the 'Congratulations! You have entered!' email was still looming in my inbox.

I needed to focus but I found it difficult; in 2016, the thought of running a marathon was never far from my thoughts and the finishing gantry was etched into my brain. For the Canal Canter Summer Extravaganza 2019 Ultra, there were only going to be 396+ runners, so I pictured the finish area being two orange traffic cones on the path. I needed something to focus on, a hook to keep me motivated, and to get rid of this cloud of doubt.

A thought that a hard copy of my training plan on the fridge might help. I used the marathon training plan I had on file, tweaked it a bit, added the new weeks' commencing dates, and empty boxes on which to manually enter the daily mileage. I used the same formula that I used for the marathon; each week increase my number of miles; on the last two weekends before the taper period, do some insane mileage – easy. Nope, it was not easy when I was full of self-doubt and lacking motivation; I was writing numbers down that looked great on paper, but I was probably not going to follow the plan.

In almost an act of desperation, I sent the first draft of my plan to Leyla, who said she would essentially hold my hand through this process. As I sent her a copy, I thought to myself, 'Leyla has no idea what she is getting herself into'. I very quickly got a reply, with many tweaks, comments, and advice. Ultimately, she tried to change my thinking about how I should train for this event: run to time and not distance.

In my research, I found that this was a highly debated topic in the running world. If person 'A' went for a 3-mile run and person 'B' went for a 35-minute run as part of their training, who's making quicker progress toward their training goal, be it a half marathon, marathon, or ultra? Without getting into the weeds and advocating one way or another, when Leyla sent me a clip of a talk given by Jack Daniels, an Olympic distance running coach about beginner runners I was convinced. Coach Daniels said,

'Your long run should be less than 25% of your weekly mileage, or 2.5 hours, whichever comes first.'

Two more quotes from the 02:31 video convinced me.

'If you run two miles a day, you could complete a 10K, no problem, right?'

True, I thought, but as we both knew, marathons and ultras were different; he went on to say,

'If you're training for a 100-mile ultra, what is your longest training run? About 30. So, you can train for 100 miles by only doing a third of the race distance and you can complete a 10K only doing a third of the distance, but for some reason you have to do 80% of the race distance to practice completing a marathon? It just doesn't make sense.'

All of this confused me. However, what I did discover was a way to avoid the 5- or 6-hour running sessions that I did when training for a marathon.

I tweaked my 20-week training plan to ensure my runs were 1, 2, or 3 hours max; stuck it to the fridge and now I was set.

All of this was done 23 weeks before the actual event, so I saw this plan every time I walked into the kitchen, which, in a way, got me motivated. Now, I just wanted to get started.

Week one was supposed to start on Monday 28th January, but as I was chomping at the bit I decided to start early. To ensure I didn't have to rejig my training plan, which was in a perfectly formatted Microsoft Excel spreadsheet, I just added a week zero in black felt tip pen at the top. My first run was a 1-hour run, during which I was able to reach the distance of 4.6 miles.

Over the following weeks, I always stopped my Garmin at the 1-, 2-, or 3-hour mark, regardless of the distance. I improved my distances in these pre-set times to reach an impressive 5.1 miles in an hour on a few occasions. At the end of the day, did I follow my plan as written? Did I heck. It all came down to time on my feet and practising running on tired legs without getting injured.

MILE 42

Finding my Focus, Training Races, and a Set Back

However you put it, 31 miles, 50 kilometres, or 50,000 meters, looks crazy, but in those numbers, I found my focus. Not in a finishing gantry, but on a finishing gadget. Keeping it simple, my focus was to see 31 miles on my Garmin, that was it. For every run, on every day, during every waking moment, this is what I thought about; this is what I visualised; this is what was seared onto the lenses and corneas of my eyes, motivating me to get out the door.

With my focus now sorted, the miles on the sheet stuck to the fridge got easier to fill in; the 25-, 29-, 32- and 39-mile weeks came and went. Most of the hours were done on weekends but I did get some solid 1-hour runs in before or after work. Mixing things up, I entered two half marathons just as training sessions. One was to be used for fuelling practice and the other for pacing practice.

The first one I entered was the 2019 North Lincs Half Marathon, an event I had run twice before. Once in 2015 (02:52:17) and again in 2016 (02:46:22), both respectable times for me. For this event, I was not looking at time; I was going to practice fuelling – when to take on fuel, how much to take on, and in what form. In the past, gels were my fuel of choice; this time I needed something more substantial, something that would take longer to break down and give me the energy to finish. Pecans, almonds, and peanut bars with added sea salt and a streak of dark chocolate down the side were the future; they tasted good and ticked all my fuelling boxes. I also wanted to introduce other potential energy sources as a test: jelly babies, crisps, and fruit.

With my test foods packed into every zipped pocket, nook, and cranny on my ultra-running vest, I was set. On the right of my chest I had one bladder bottle filled with water and on the left a bladder bottle filled with an electrolyte drink. Being physically, and emotionally set, my goal for this race was to practise fuelling. What I also did pre-race was research some energy conservation techniques; for approaching hills, I found this motto that I still live by now: 'If you can't see the top, then walk'. This was to make sure you felt fresh enough to finish a race strong and with energy to spare, which is exactly what I needed to do.

Flashing forward to mile 9 on this training run, my usual bad practice of starting off too fast was apparent, When I reached this point my legs became tree trunks … again. When will I ever bloody learn? The cloud of ultra-doubt returned. I should have felt fresh, confident, and awake. In reality, I felt like shit.

The end of this terrible training run was approaching, and with 400 meters to go, I started my sprint finish.

'Why am I doing a sprint finish?' I asked myself.

'This race was all about ultra-practice, not getting a good time.'

I didn't even consider the pace for this race, but even with the fuelling and energy conservation setbacks, I felt I had run at a good pace. As my plan for today's run was in tatters, maybe – just maybe – I could achieve a North Lincs PB. The finishing gantry clock came into focus; the timer said 02:58:10 and was quickly ticking towards 3 hours.

'What the hell? Coming up to 3 hours? I thought I was doing a good pace!'

This is when the second sprint finish started; I now wanted to finish in under 3 hours.

I finished in 02:59:23 with nothing left in the tank to continue; the ultra-doubt cloud had become blacker at week 14 of my training plan.

As part of my training, for the following weekend I had entered the second and last official race before the ultra – the 2019 Leeds Half Marathon. This one was kind of special. Following the 2005 and 2008 Leeds Half Marathons, for which I was instrumental in organising (if I do say so myself), I felt it was, once again, a full circle moment – a type of metaphorical 'cherry on the cake' scenario in which I was now able to experience the race from the other side of the barriers. Being a part of the organising staff for such a large event with, at the time 5,000 runners, I always had an appreciation for what when into running these events (no pun intended). The sponsor tents, metal barriers, water stations, finishing funnels, pace car, medals, t-shirts, goodie bags, Saint John's Ambulance, the road closures, the police, the entertainment, Portaloos, and, of course, the volunteers all had to be recruited, negotiated, set up, ordered, designed, organised, and coordinated. It was nice to see the race day unfold in front of me and not have any responsibility for its orchestration this time.

The start of the race was no different than any other run; the only thing different was my focus. With fuelling practice still a working progress, this race was to be used to practise pace, and at the last minute, I decided to practise energy conservation again. My goal was to keep pace consistent and have enough energy at the end of the race to run to my car, which I parked two miles away on purpose. This would subconsciously ensure I kept enough energy in reserve. What a brilliant idea, right?

Race warmups with their over-enthusiastic aerobics instructors always intrigued me. Even though we were in the starting funnel, packed in like sardines, people still tried to do the grapevine to the right, knee lifts, arm circles, and lunges. I can appreciate it's all about the atmosphere but just don't bend down to tie your shoelace during the group warm up; you might get a black eye. I usually stick by the barrier and wait; this time, I did a very slight calf stretch using the bottom of the race barrier as leverage. I was set; it was 9:00am and the race had started.

'Don't start of too fast; maintain a slow pace to conserve energy', was my mantra for the day.

As the start horn sounded, I passed the medals hanging on the metal frame and thought,

'That's going to look good on my medal rack.'

I crossed the starting mat, pushed the button on my Garmin, pushed the play button on my music and was all set, so I thought.

I was jockeying for position as you do at the start of any race in which there are lots of people. At 0.3 of a mile, there was a sharp pain in my left calf; it hurt – it bloody hurt. I limped to the sidewalk and stopped. It felt like my calf muscle had contracted and was not releasing. I rubbed it and the muscle was hard to the touch. I thought a quick stretch would do the trick and I tried to set off running again, no chance! The gastrocnemius muscle was in full lock down or full contraction.

'What the hell? An injury? I never get injured!' I actually said out loud.

I couldn't move; any weight on my foot would cause a jolt of pain to sear through the centre of my calf.

Some race marshals approached and asked,

'Are you ok?'

'Umm, I'm not sure.' I said willing my muscle to release.

I muttered under my breath,

'I never get bloody injured!'

The marshals returned to their post as I waved them off.

I was not moving from this spot. People were passing me by, as I stood there helpless, embarrassed, and feeling very sorry for myself. I tried to walk but the pain was now worse, the muscle was so tight that any movement caused excruciating pain. Then it happened; a decision had to be made.

'Are you dropping out?' The trail marshal asked with authority.

'I guess?' I said in the form of a question followed by,

'I really can't believe it, I never get….'.

This follow marshal wasn't bothered; he was on the radio before I even finished speaking.

'Number 4974 has withdrawn', he relayed to a voice on the other end of the radio. I could have sworn I heard the reply,

'Really?'

Just like that, the thought of finishing the Leeds Half Marathon and this full circle moment was over, but a new challenge had begun – I needed to get back to the start to see if the paramedics could help me understand what the hell had just happened.

It was like a walk of shame, I had to walk against the flow of people who had just watched their loved ones and friends start their 13.1-mile journey. I was limping helplessly back to the start like a wounded animal, mere seconds after the race had started. To say I felt humiliated would have been an understatement. It may have only taken me less than three minutes from the start to the spot at which my injury occurred, but it took me 39 minutes to get back to the start and the first aid tent.

I self-consciously walked into the makeshift tent; the paramedics looked at me with surprise and concern. I told them what had happened, no tear, no pop, no strain – it just contracted and stayed contracted without warning or reason. They felt the muscle for heat, no heat; inspected it for swelling, no swelling. Nothing, just a tight calf muscle that would not release.

I was ashamed, uncomfortable, self-conscious, and abashed. Then the colour quickly drained from my face and I felt almost transparent as I realised that I now had a 2-mile limp back to my car. That trek, in fact, took me 90 minutes. Who the hell's idea was that!? Why not get an Uber you might be thinking? Well, with all the road closures, it would have been a 2-hour wait. Trust me. I looked into all the options.

Three weeks before taper, I had an injury that put my ultra in jeopardy. For the following week I was fixated on making it better quickly. In a few days, it did get better, but not 'ready to run on' better. People on Facebook pleaded with me to rest, but I needed to do something; after all, I was running 50K in 5 weeks.

MILE 43

Think of the Children

With this injury I now had an out; I could, in fact, pull out of the ultra. People drop out of races all the time because of injury and, at this point, it was a serious consideration. It felt as if all the fitness capital I had built up was leaving my body with every passing day. I tried a lane swim just to keep my fitness up, but it just didn't feel right. On the Friday following my DNF on that Sunday, I finally felt able to venture out for a short, light run with what felt like a 'charley horse' in the left calf. As it hurt only mildly following that run, I then attempted another 3 miles on the Saturday, giving me a 5-mile total for week 16. The injury could have gone either way during these runs; lucky for me it was a positive outcome that enabled me to get back on track. During week 17, I built up a total of 29.7 carefully run miles.

Why did I not just throw in the towel? The answer to that is easy – my family. Ross and Tasha knew the big event was getting close and every now and then they would ask,

'Dad, is it this weekend you are doing your ultra?'

It was the way they asked that caught my attention. I got a sense that they were proud, happy, and content that their dad had a goal and was doing something remarkable. Maybe I was way off base in analysing how they spoke, but I did hear them both tell their friends over Xbox live while playing Fortnight,

'My dad's running an ultra.'

That was enough for me.

MILE 44

The Dreaded Final Training Run

On the Saturday of week 17, it said I was to do one 2-hour run in the morning and a second 2-hour run in the evening. This was not happening. I had done two or three double up sessions during my training, but I had entered full panic mode and all rational thought went out of the window. I wasn't feeling confident that I had done enough, physically or mentally, to finish 50K. I really needed to get a big run in; a run that would help get rid of this cloud of doubt. So, against all the advice I was given, I decided to do what I did when I was training for the marathon in 2016, a 22-miler for my last training run before taper time. This run would either break me or empower me.

I took three days off running to prepare myself. I wasn't really sure of a good route. I couldn't do the same route as in 2016 as we'd moved to a new house. I had also, more importantly, promised never to run past those structures on that route again. So, my thought process told me to run along the main road to Wakefield, which had a pavement for 11 miles, then turn around: easy peasy!

The 22-miler day was 1st June 2019. I wore everything I was going to wear on ultra-day and I was carrying everything I planned to carry; it was a kind of dress rehearsal. Pace, fuelling, and energy conservation were all at the forefront of my mind.

One foot in front of the other, and after 53,500 steps, I should be done, right? Well sure. During this slog I walked, I ran, and I walked some more. At the halfway mark there was a petrol station at which I reloaded my energy bars and then returned home; it all went to plan. It went so well and I had conserved so much energy that I even tried to make the last mile of this training run the fastest. The fastest mile during this run was 14:29 (mile 2), my average pace for the entire run was 16:03, and my pace for the 22nd mile was 14:39: unbelievable! According to Strava, I ran 22.31 miles in 05:57:58 and I was chuffed. With some quick maths, I figured I would have achieved a marathon PB if I had tried, but I was not silly enough to run a marathon just for the hell of it – that would have been sheer folly.

My brain and body were in sync and my confidence was high. I could now relax and enjoy my favourite part of training – taper. The only downer on this day was during the long run, my thoughts had turned to the hot tub that we had rented for Tasha's 10th birthday party for her and her giggling besties. It was going to be glorious sitting in a hot tub basking in the magnificence of the fact that all the training had paid off and that I was ready. When I got back to the house, I threw all gadgets aside, removed my shoes and fell backward into the hot tub with all my running gear on. As the water engulfed my aching body I was shocked to discover that the heater had been turned off overnight and the water was now freezing cold. I now found myself soaked, trembling, and asking myself: was this a warning of things to come?!

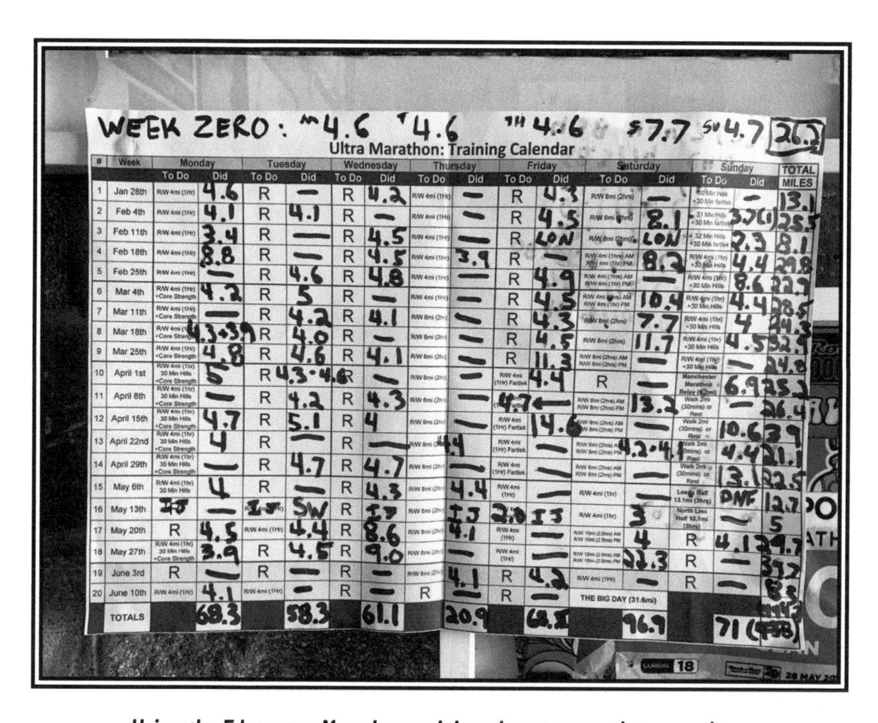

Using the Edmonton Marathon training plan as a template, my ultra-marathon training plan was created. As you can see, I was so eager to get started that I added a week zero to the top of the sheet. Not only did it record my runs, it also became a piece of artwork on my fridge (now in my Man Cave): something Strava could never be.

MILE 45

The Pain Before the Real Pain

Taper time is magnificent; not having to run after a 39.7-mile week was a relief. Time to recover, reflect, and rejoice. My calf injury was still on my mind; it didn't hurt but maybe I needed it looked at. Killing two birds with one stone, I thought I would treat (with a small t) myself to a pre-race sports massage. With a quick text to my sports massage guy John Hackleton, I was in luck; there was an opening the Tuesday prior to the big race. I hadn't seen John in a while, but knew he could educate me on what the issue was with my calf.

I told him the story of what happened but John admitted he had been watching my progress on Facebook and Strava. John was going to start with the calves and see how much work they needed. John mistakenly assumed that I had seen other sports masseurs since I had seen him last.

'John, you're my guy! I haven't been to see anyone since we last met', I stated, placing my head in the hole in the table.

John checked his notes,

'You mean you haven't seen anyone else since? The last time I saw you was in 2016', he said, sounding concerned.

'Ya, after my Marathon. When I got back from Canada.' I said, not able to read his reaction.

'Oh my!' John said awkwardly.

I was looking at the floor, but I pictured him rolling up his sleeves and eager to dig in.

John's 'Oh my', soon changed to 'Oh boy', as he placed his fingers on my left calf.

'This is going to hurt', John said, apologetically.

Before I could reply, John dug his fingers into my calf. I gripped the table tightly with both hands as my body convulsed, just as if a doctor had shouted, 'Clear!'

'That's not good', I thought. I repeated those words out loud, many times.

It was like John was a ninja. He knew where all the pressure points were to incapacitate a man. I shook, lurched, quaked, and grunted with pain with every pass over my calf muscles.

'I'm not even touching you, Sean.' John said, with laughing concern.

The next words out of his mouth shook me to my core.

'Sean, I honestly can't believe how tight your calf muscles are; with all the miles you've done, I'm surprised nothings ever happened to you. Do you get pain around your ankle?'

'Yup', I said in between groans.

'Do you get soreness or pain on the bottom of your foot?

'All the time', I said.

'Well, it's because your calf is so tight. I'm not surprised you're in so much pain now! Do you stretch after your runs?' he asked, already knowing the answer.

'Ahhh...'

'Well you should!' John said before I could answer.

He then moved to the other calf and said, 'this one feels worse.'

'Do you have a stick I can bite down on', I asked jokingly, but secretly wished he did.

John went on to say at least eight more times, the following statements:

'Oh my, your muscles are tight.'

'You really need to stretch after your runs.'

'I can't believe you haven't seen anybody for three years.'

And my favourite ...

'I'm really surprised you haven't been injured yet.'

I reminded him that I was injured, just a few weeks ago, but then went on to ask him two very important questions.

'Could my tight calf muscles all of a sudden be pulled, or worse, tear? Could it happen during a really, really long run? Let's say a 50K?'

'Potentially, but I'm sure it might not happen.' He said in a non-committal, double negative word salad.

Great, I thought to myself. I now had two grenades attached to my calves and the pins could fall out at any minute.

'I don't think I am going to have time to get to your IT band today Sean', John said in a way that almost sounded like relief.

The iliotibial or IT band is a thick band of connective tissue that runs from the outside of your hip to the outside of the knee. If not stretched properly or often, it can lead to iliotibial band syndrome (also known as IT band syndrome). It is one of the most common overuse injuries among runners and occurs when the IT band is tight or inflamed.

I shot back quickly, 'I don't want you anywhere near my IT band', knowing that I stretched that less than my calves.

The experience was painful but needed. As expected, the next day my legs felt heavy. What I didn't expect was how sore they were to touch. Knowing I still had three more days until the ultra, I hoped they would have recovered by then. As a side note, I did promise John that I would book a monthly appointment to ensure I took care of myself, and that was a promise I intended to keep, regardless of the outcome of the ultra.

MILE 46

The 2019 Canal Canter Summer Extravaganza (50K Ultra Marathon)

After 21 weeks of training, 471 miles, and 1,919 days since I left my house for my first run in 2014, the time had come. I was about to run an ultra-marathon.

Over the last few weeks, a lot of activity had happened behind the scenes via emails between the race organisers at 'It's Grim Up North Running' and myself. As it was a very small event, they had imposed a time limit. I knew I would be outside this limit and was able to negotiate a 90-minute head start. However, even with a head start I knew it would be close, so I just wanted to ensure that I would get a medal by reiterating in several emails that I was slow, and if the volunteers had to be pulled in and everything needed to be packed up while I was still running, I gave them permission to leave my medal hanging from a branch at the finishing area.

During the last weeks leading up to the big day, Leyla and I kept in touch intermittently via Facebook messenger. Whenever I had a question, she would reply within minutes, giving me advice, words of encouragement, and ultra-tips.

At this point, there was no more time for questions, prep, or doubt. Leyla was picking me up at 7:00am. I was up at 5:00am, not in a panic, but in a surprisingly calm mood and in bed by myself. Where was Wendy you might ask? Well, that's a story in itself!

In August 2018, at the tail end of a family trip to Belfast and while I was flying home to go back to work, the rest of the family, along with my mum, stayed a few extra days. They had booked a trip to the Giant's Causeway, where Wendy literally found herself stuck between a rock and a hard place when she fell, severely damaging her left foot. Upon her return to the UK, it never fully healed. She had seen several doctors, specialist, and consultants, who eventually realised that she needed to undergo an operation. To cut a long story short, her operation was scheduled two days before the ultra, which meant she would not be at the finish line and she would have to sleep downstairs in the room my mum used when she came to visit. It was disappointing, but I knew she would've been there if she could.

Miles, my imaginary running man, was not lying on the floor waiting for me to dismantle him; a pile of pre-selected running gear was just folded nicely on the window ledge. It was almost as if Miles had grown up and moved out; it was years since I had laid my running gear out in the form of a person. Each piece of running gear was run tested and washed. As I was putting it on, I said to myself,

'I'm just going for a long run today.'

I started with my underwear, then socks, my short sleeved compression top, my lucky Nike running tights (yup, no baggy shorts), and, finally, my Canada t-shirt to finish off the ensemble. Something didn't feel right; I reached down to feel a massive hole in the crotch area. My lucky Nike running tights had ripped – oh crap! I tried to stay positive; I was not superstitious and it was only a minor setback as I had other tights to choose from. 'At least it didn't happen while I was running', I thought to myself.

My Ultimate Distance hydration vest had been pre-filled with 13 tried-and-tested energy bars, electrolyte tablets, were pre-wrapped individually in tinfoil and my usual porridge pots were ready to be filled with hot water. While the oats were stewing, I ensured all the paperwork was available and the directions and maps to the venue were tucked away safely. Upon returning to my porridge oats, they didn't look or smell right; they were clumping into gelatinous lumps that did NOT look edible. They had to be thrown out. I then had to use my back up breakfast: raisin toast, Weetabix, skimmed milk, and a few bananas. Was this going to sustain me like a good old bowl of steaming porridge oats would? I bloody hope so. That was two things that didn't go to plan; what was the third going to be?

I was all set and now pacing back and forth in the kitchen, waiting for Leyla. After a quick, 'Good luck luv,' from Wendy in her makeshift hospital bed, followed by a 'Please bring my husband home safe,' aimed at Leyla, who had just arrived and was now standing in the doorway, we were on our way.

'Have you any idea what you've got yourself into?' I asked Leyla.

This was the way I started every conversation we had about her running the ultra with me. What followed had been said at least nine times and I am sure she was sick of having the following conversation, but I just wanted to be sure, one last time.

Before she could reply, I continued.

'I'm slow.'

'It's going to be tough for you to run at my pace; it's almost three times slower than the pace you're used to.'

'Have you ever run a 14-hour ultra?

'It will be fine, Sean. I will go at your pace and it doesn't matter how slow you go.'

After about 30 minutes of nervous small talk and silence we had arrived.

The race headquarters looked like a hole in the wall; it was a pub located in what seemed to be a shady part of Leeds. It was just a guess, but looking at the graffiti, barbed wire, and bars on the windows of adjacent buildings, it looked like people were preparing for the 'Purge', so I was probably right. Being early, there were only a few cars in the parking lot, with even fewer people hanging about.

There were several events on the day, all with different start times. A 5K, 10K, Half Marathon, 20-miler, and the 50K Ultra. To make it clear which runners were running in each event, the race numbers all had different colours. Our colour was red; my race number was 9 and Leyla's was 7. There were only a few numbers left on the pile where the ultra-runners registered. Then it hit me; there were just over 400 people registered to run today and I suddenly realised that not all of them would be running the ultra. I asked a marshal how many runners were there for the ultra ... the answer was 11.

It was daft of me to think that all 400 runners were running the ultra, but only 11? I thought 679 in the marathon was bad, but this was so much worse. My heart sank. Was this the third thing that was not going to plan today? We got a lift to the start line as it was about 1K away. The start area was unlike any I had ever seen. There were maybe 8 to 12 people milling around, setting things up and doing all the prep. The start line wasn't even marked with cones as I envisioned; there were just three timing mats set across a thin path.

Leyla took charge at this point; maybe she saw the terror on my face or the fact I looked completely out of my depth. She explained the route to me.

'We will be starting with a 10K (6.2 mile) out and back to the start area; then we'll do a 30K (20 mile) out and back, then repeat the original 10K out and back for a grand total of 50K or 31 miles … ish'

'Ish …', I pondered, but I didn't ask for clarity.

Leyla also explained that, because we were starting early, there were no marshals out yet, so the race director's instructions to her were then relayed to me. We needed to run to about 3.1 miles, then turn around and run back. I didn't have time to think about the laissez-faire attitude they had toward the distances as it was now 8:30am and time to set off.

As the other runners were to start at 10:00am, there was no over-enthusiastic aerobics instructor doing a warmup, no music, not even a horn, just three timing mats and a non-existent pre-race atmosphere, which I wasn't used to. It was just Leyla and me standing there, looking at the long path ahead. Well, it wasn't a path; it was a trail. Did I mention this race was billed as a trail ultra? I despised trail running; I was a turned ankle away from retiring from running all together. Don't get me wrong, many of my running friends love trail running, including Leyla. However, in every trail-run narrative there was almost always an anecdote of how they could have been injured, hopping over tree roots, avoiding gopher holes, and shoes getting left in mud as they crossed a stream – not for me!

This race was along a canal and, during my research, I found that most of the surface was paved, some was on shale, and a very small part was on cobbles and rocks, so I could live with that.

Without a fanfare, we were off, and as we started we both slid into a 13:01 minute mile which was a tad fast for me, so we eased into a slower 14:44 pace for the next few miles. I was tracking distance in miles, Leyla was tracking in kilometres so, from the start, we were speaking a different language. Leyla's rationale for using kilometres was that they were shorter than miles, so psychologically, it felt you were going faster as the numbers went up in more rapid succession. I had never thought of that, as I didn't do the number of weekly miles she did. We then found ourselves debating my Garmin running watch vs her Suunto. It was all in good fun and it passed the time.

Nobody was on the path; we were alone. In the canal, the water reflected the trees and the medieval wall on our right. Leyla was pondering what was behind that wall and asked me a rhetorical question,

'What do you think that wall and those pipes were used for?'

I looked up, seeing the wall for the first time as I was in a focus bubble, putting one foot in front of the other, unaware of my surroundings.

'I don't know.' I replied in between breaths.

3.1 miles appeared on my watch,

'What does your watch say?' I asked to confirm the distance.

'5K' she replied.

'I guess we can turn around.' I said with relief.

For me, in an out and back race, the back is better; knowing that you're on your way home is satisfying.

The strategy that I was planning to use today, was to break the race into 4-mile chunks. Every 4 miles was about an hour in training, plus, in my mind's eye, I knew exactly where I would be if I was running my local 4-mile run. This way, I could visualise where I was and how far I had to run. As a bonus, running 15-minute miles would ensure I had enough energy to finish. With no scientific theory to attach this to, it was just a strategy I needed to use to ensure the thought of 50k would not overwhelm me.

However, knowing there were three out and backs, my strategy changed slightly. I swapped it to the mindset that each specific out and back was a goal within a goal. Goal one had been achieved and there were just another 3.1 miles to the next milestone.

The surfaces on this first part changed between sharp protruding rocks and uneven cobbles, to shale, then a paved path. As we got closer to the start area, the surface returned to protruding rocks and uneven cobbles.

I could see people assembled together at the start area. As it took us just under 90 minutes to do the first 10K, it was very close to the time all the other runners were to start. As we reached the start area, we were cheered and clapped across the three timing mats. It felt a bit weird and awkward to me, clapping for somebody who was so slow and needed to start earlier than the rest, For some reason, it made me feel a bit uncomfortable. However, thinking about it now, the cheers and claps were the running community as a whole supporting one of its own, and I should have been more grateful at the time.

Now we were about to start the longest part of the run, a 20-miler out and back. I had a plan; get to 10 miles, as it was only 4 miles away. I visualised leaving my house and going for my standard 1-hour run. The canal was filling up with long canal boats and I saw some early morning ramblers when I occasionally popped my head out of my focus bubble.

Yes, Leyla was still with me, speeding up and slowing down; at one point she even ran backwards, to which I then jokingly said,

'Now you're just showing off.'

It was at the 8-mile mark that I picked up on the fact that Leyla had been trying to start a conversation with me as we ran. My replies we usually, yup, really, not sure or a knowing nod, and an eyebrow raising facial gesture usually did the trick. It must be very frustrating, running at one third your pace and trying to start a conversation to pass the time with somebody who just mumbled between heavy breathing. I'm not sure at what point it was that she started to regret agreeing to run with me and I'm sure she will never admit that she did, but I sensed that it was just before we hit the 10-mile mark.

As I was not in a chatty mood, she found other ways to pass the time. She was giving Wendy real time updates via Facebook messenger and posting photos of my progress on Facebook for all to see.

We had hit a few water stations along the way, which consisted of about 8 to 12 half-filled small plastic cups with water or diluted squash on the corner of a square folding card table – the type of table you'd see at a car boot sale, covered in cheap tat. They also had a large plastic bladder filled with water, which I used to fill my water bottles. I would unwrap one of my individually wrapped electrolyte tablets and plop it into the left bottle attached to my chest. There were also a few feed stations on the route. However, in my head I was expecting several large bowls and platters of jelly babies, pizzas, fries, an assortment of other junk food and confectionary goods that could be used to refuel a runner. I assumed this because of the refuelling stations I had only read about on these international ultra-routes. Subconsciously, I was just hoping for such a spread, so that I could get a break from my dry maple syrup pecan and peanut bars.

As I arrived at these feed stations, what I saw was almost the opposite of what I had imagined. There were even fewer plastic cups than on the water stations. There was only one open snack-sized pack of ready salted Walkers crisps; the size I put in my kid's lunch. There was a small bag of Liquorice Allsorts, and, yes there were jelly babies but only eight, as the other runners who, at this point, had passed me had the first crack at picking their favourites. It looked like it was expected that we were to share what was on the table, which was a shame as I could have devoured its entire contents; however, I thought that this might not be proper ultra-etiquette.

My legs were getting tired and it worried me; my pace dropped to 17-minute miles as we crossed the half marathon point (another milestone that I had set for myself). This was not good, I was flagging with so many more miles to go. I then thought of something that might just give me that second wind, music.

Prior to the race I had set up several different playlists of the usual high-energy club mixes that would keep me motivated. I would have started the race with my music as I did with every run, but at the start of the race I was conflicted. What kind of friend would I have been to a person whom I respected and who was sacrificing her Saturday away from her family to run with me, if I had put my headphones in? If I had done that, I wouldn't have talked to Leyla at all during the run. Well, if I'm honest, I hadn't talked to her for the last three hours anyway, due to my damn focus bubble. I assessed the situation and, like a selfish jackass, I tentatively announced,

'Leyla, I think what I need to get me going faster is a bit of music.'

'Out loud or in ear music?' she replied.

I selfishly said, in the form of a question,

'In ear music?' I knew it was wrong, but I needed to get rid of this doubt cloud that was moving in fast.

If Leyla didn't regret this run at mile 10, she definitely did at mile 14. The music did not last long, due to the pathway getting busier with walkers, bikers and other runners who had caught up to us. As I was listening to Queen's *Don't Stop Me Now*, Leyla looked at me as if she wanted to tell me something, so I took out an earphone and then quickly realised Leyla was gesturing that a bike was coming up behind me. The music idea only lasted for 17 minutes.

Sensing her frustration, I tried to open a dialogue as we had walked the last few miles. I was trying to explain my incoherent milestone strategy,

'I wanted to get to 10-miles, then 13.1, then 20, then 22-miles as that would equal the longest run of the year, 23-miles because that's my favourite number.'

Leyla interrupted,

'Your overthinking it; just take one mile at a time and enjoy it. You're doing great and you're going to be an ultra-runner after today!'

She said this, as if to say,

'Finally! A conversation!'

'You're right, I am over thinking it and I'm struggling. Or am I struggling because I'm over thinking it?' I asked profoundly, not expecting an answer.

We had reached the turnaround point, 16.2 miles. With just under 4 miles to my next milestone, I held back eating everything on the table; either my fuelling practice was paying off or I didn't have the energy to eat.

On the 'back' run it was so satisfying to know that we were on our way back to the finish. By now we were only doing 19- to 20-minute miles and my feet were swelling so much I had to loosen the laces. Leyla was being optimistic while, again, updating Wendy and putting updates on Facebook. Leyla then relayed all the positive well wishes to me, which, at this point were just ricocheting off the wall of doubt that I was building around me. I was in a bad place and I felt it was only going to get worse.

'How the hell am I going to finish this? This is not going to end well, Leyla', I said, defeated and feeling very sorry for myself.

'You are going to do this, Sean. I've got your back and you WILL finish!' Leyla replied.

Then it all just poured out …

'Just look at how slow we are going … this is crap. You must be so frustrated. I am walking faster than I run and it's still taking 23 minutes to do a mile.'

'Then we walk it; it doesn't matter how long it takes', Leyla proclaimed

'Do you mean, if somebody walks 50K, they would be considered an ultra-marathoner?' I asked, really interested in the answer.

'Yup!' Leyla fired back without hesitation.

I squinted my left eye, curled my nose and rubbed my chin pondering if that was, in fact, true. Surely you should run an ultra, or at least most of it, to call yourself an ultra-marathon.

Leyla's pep talk did the trick; I started to run again announcing I was having my 7th wind.

At mile 20 I had an internal celebration, but we were back to walking. In the distance, I saw a familiar face – Jase Windu was running toward us. Leyla announced his arrival by saying,

'Look who's here!'

Jase was a friend who had participated in a few of my silly challenges in the past, and if you looked at his Strava it looked like he ran everywhere. He was a solid friend who would do anything for you. This was evident when Leyla texted him to join me in my quest.

The optimist in me would say,

'It's great that Jase is happy to take a big chunk of time out of his day to support me in becoming an ultra-marathon runner!'

The pessimist in me would say,

'It's great that Jase is happy to take a big chunk of time out of his day to support Leyla, while she endures this relentless task of helping a friend who doesn't talk while running, to become an ultra-marathoner.'

At the end of the day, I think it was a bit of both, and I did really appreciate him showing up.

At mile 22, I once again had an internal celebration because it matched the longest run of the year, but I was struggling more than ever. My feet were still swelling, meaning that I had to loosen my laces even more.

With all this going on, at exactly 23.9 miles, the third thing that didn't go as planned today reared its ugly head. My Garmin running watch ran out of battery. I freaked out and the first thing that I thought was, if it was not on Strava it never happened. I was lost for words; I could actually only find one word – FUCK! This really caught me out and I started to panic, my incoherent ramblings became worse and worse. It was like my brain and body threw in the towel. I said,

'That's it! Nothing to see here. It was a waste of 20 weeks of training; nothing to show for it; it never happened; move along!'

'Do you have your phone with you?' Jase asked, putting his hand on my shoulder to calm me down as I really was in a right state.

After Jase's prompt, I remembered that Strava would work on my phone. Even with this great idea at hand, I still returned to having a ridiculous internal argument with myself.

'It wouldn't be the entire run on one activity, it would be a bit like Frankenstein having to put two runs together.' This illogical, jumbled, and irrational moment of the race must have pushed Jase and Leyla over the edge. After I handed Jase my phone, he adjusted the settings and got it working; I had never actually used Strava on my phone before. From that point on, Jase and Leyla walked ahead of me, leaving me to continue my disjointed conversation I was having with myself – I had lost it.

I was now relying on Leyla's Suunto running watch, at which point she reminded me about our debate about which running watch was better, by telling me her watch was still at 70%.

Soon after, Leyla announced that we had reached 42.1 kilometres. As I was in a fog of pain and frustration and could not convert kilometres into miles, I didn't know what that meant.

Leyla clarified it for me by announcing, 'We've finished the marathon!'

I was happy, then confused, then angry.

'Wait a minute, we are at least 3 to 4 kilometres from the start area! How the hell could we have finished the marathon? We still need to do a 10K when we get back to the start, right? What does that mean? We can't have done a marathon. What's the time?'

'07:37:54.' Leyla said, knowing what was coming next.

I was fuming, not thinking straight and flew completely off the handle.

'Well, that is a shite time for me; well over 30 minutes past my marathon PB time!' In the moment I didn't realise that this was actually a perfect ultra-pace, but I continued my incoherent rant.

'Do you mean to tell me we still have to get to the start area, however the hell long that's going to take us? Then we have ANOTHER 10K? This distance should count toward the 10K we have to do. That means we are going to have to do more than 50K! HOW THE HELL DOES THAT WORK?!'

Leyla tried to explain, knowing I was a powder keg of emotion.

'As it's a small event all distances are 'ish', they don't officially measure the distances. The start area is there because cars can be parked. The turnaround points are also basically where the volunteers can park their cars. They approximate what the distances will be.'

In my present state, I was not having it; this distance debate was not over. I had run a marathon and I didn't enjoy the moment. Instead, I took my frustration out on Leyla – both barrels. This foolish behaviour on my part lasted for the next hour. We had come to the bridge that was just before the start area. By this time, we had walked/slogged 44K and still had 10K to go. I rounded the final turn at the pace of a 24-minute mile to see the start area in all its anti-glory. What I heard next pushed me into a whole new level of irritation.

'Are you continuing?' someone yelled from a group of people milling around near the finishing tent.

I wasn't sure who asked the question, but one of the main organisers emerged from the pack to ask the question again.

'Are you carrying on?' she asked.

'You bet!' I said, 'I've got an extra-long ultra to run!' I snapped back.

'Well I cannot allow that; it's past the cut off time and we are going to have to ask you to stop running', she replied while the medals were being packed away.

I froze. I looked at her with a wide-eyed steely stare and my left eye twitched. I walked towards her so we were almost nose-to-nose. Sweat was rolling down my red face, not from the run but from the rage boiling inside me. I paused and said, through gritted teeth, using every ounce of reserve energy I could muster …

'I am no chicken – I AM A FOX!!'

The marshal looked at me as if to say, "What the hell are you talking about? What chicken? What fox?"

I had always admired the fox and the chicken and what they did when the marshal stopped them during the Manchester Marathon. Could I have done what the fox did? Well today, I became the fox and like that woman three years earlier, I was not taking any shit.

Before I could fill my lungs with air to continue, Leyla, who knew my history of being stopped, jumped in before I said something I would probably later regret.

'We are going to continue.' Leyla said emphatically, now standing between me and the lady.

'That's no problem, but there won't be any marshals for you on the course', she said, thinking that was going to stop us.

At this point, Jase stepped in as well, double blocking me and literally covering my mouth and stopping me from yelling what I wanted to say.

'We didn't have marshals when we started, so we will be fine' Leyla retorted.

'Ok, but please take my number and text me when you're finished; I just want to know you finished safe'. With that reply, we were back on track.

Leyla had warned me about an adrenalin rush that she hoped would help me finish the race. I am not sure this was what she had in mind, but adrenalin definitely hit the blood stream.

This adrenalin rush very quickly turn to emotion; as I started my last 10K, I saw Ross and Tasha sitting on a bench. My father-in-law had brought them to see me finish. All the anger, irritation, fog, and anxiety evaporated; I grabbed my kids and gave them a big hug.

'You're here!' I yelled with an overwhelming sense of relief.

We chatted, I told them the story so far and that I still needed to do 10K, so they didn't have to wait. I hugged them again and went on to finish this damn ultra – for them. In a matter of just a few minutes, I went from irrational, irritated, and emotional, to … wet. Yes, the skies opened, and we were now in the middle of what felt like a typhoon. The rain was coming down hard, and as Leyla was sorting the medals, I found this new level of determination that superseded all expectation. I started to run and I was running fast.

This was a weird moment. Minutes after I became the "Fox" and just before I started the last 6.2 miles of the ultra, my father-in-law surprised me by bringing the kids to support me. It was an emotional four minutes. It truly gave me the boost I needed to continue. I just love this picture; looking at Tasha and Ross, I almost see that same pride that I saw in their faces during the Blackpool Half Marathon.

I'm not sure if it was the adrenalin or the emotion from seeing my kids, but in hindsight it was probably a bit of both. I was motoring for what felt like a good five minutes and when Leyla and Jase finally caught up, I asked what's our pace? Jase looked at his watch and said 13:10, the fastest pace of the day, even after I had just run 44K. As my Brooks Glycerine 18s splashed through the large puddles that were forming quickly on the path, I thought I may have been able to run faster sooner if I had had this amount of energy in reserve. It didn't last. I like to think I maintained that speed for a mile; realistically, it was just less than half a kilometre.

After this surge, my body and mind were finally in sync; however, it was not to run and finish, it was to stop and revolt. My mind and body said,

'A strong finish to this ultra would have been a great end to your book, Sean, but you still have 10K to finish and we are going on strike, effective immediately.'

Both my mind and body literally quit working and shut down. This WAS the WALL; I knew this as I'd never EVER felt this way at ANY point in my running career, EVER. I guess I should be grateful that I'd never hit the wall before, because it may have stopped me doing any challenges; but I digress.

Every limb attached to my body, starting with my feet, just stopped working. In addition, the fact that I had been loosening my shoes so much had now caused friction there was now friction between the sole of my shoe, the two pairs of socks I wore as standard, and my foot. It was at this point I experienced the real runner's wall; all of the other 'walls' that I thought I had hit in other races were infinitesimal in comparison to what I was experiencing right now. Due to friction, two humongous running blisters had appeared, one on each foot, whom I later named Nunzio and Pasquali. My grenade calves that John warned me about lost their respective pins and exploded. The blood drained from my face. I became dizzy and couldn't see straight; my arms felt like I was holding two industrial-sized sledgehammers, one in each hand. Oh … and there were snipers – all aimed at me; the snipers David Lee talked about. There were so many it felt like I was in the opening scene of Saving Private Ryan. I was done; this wall was behemoth and it just fell on me. The only thing, and I really do mean the ONLY thing stopping me from collapsing, was one thought; 50K on the watch.

We were fast approaching 28-minute miles when I asked how many kilometres we had left to go.

Leyla answered '6'. Jase added, 'ish'. I was NOT amused.

My ranting soon returned,

'I'm only doing the 50K, as advertised. Let's just turn around to ensure we only do 50k' I pleaded.

'You'll kick yourself for not finishing the entire race.' Leyla countered.

I was relentless,

'We haven't even reached the turnaround point for this 10K, it's going to be hours. I am in absolute pain.' I whined like a 12-year old, being told he needed to come off Fortnight in the middle of a Battle Royal.

Leyla and Jase now had a new strategy for dealing with me – walk so far ahead that I was out of ear shot.

It took forever, but we reached the turnaround point and were now on our way back. At this point, even though we were on the back run of an out and back, there was no joy in the fact. I was in desperate bad shape; I was dizzy, shuffling, and moving from one side of the path to the other. I must have looked like one of those slow walkers on The Walking Dead; I sure as hell felt like one.

As I lumbered slowly, Leyla and Jase had stopped ahead. It took a while, but I caught up with them. Leyla extended her arm to show me something on her wrist. It took time for me to focus, but her watch said 50K. I tried to process what I saw; was I hallucinating? Was I dreaming? Or was it the real thing? After about three minutes it hit me; I had done it! Even though the rain had stopped by now, the water works started again, not from the sky, but from my eyes; I started to sob. Not the gulp crying I did when I finished the Marathon; this was just quiet sobbing. Tears of joy, accomplishment, and relief because I had just achieved something I thought was absolutely out of reach … again.

I grabbed Leyla's wrist and in between the sobs, I quietly said,

'Thank you … you believed in me even when I didn't believe in myself. I could not have done this without you.'

Leyla put the ultra-medal around my neck hugged me and said,

'Congratulations, and welcome to the club.'

My happy accomplishment tears turned to sadness because of how I had treated both Leyla and Jase. My snapping, abruptness, and inappropriate behaviour was harsh and they didn't deserve it. I hugged them both again and said I was sorry.

That moment of the race will be the one I remember the most and will keep me humble. It was the person I became during this run that was to be the main reason I didn't attempt another. That wasn't me; it wasn't right. As my mind returned to the here and now, we still had 4K to finish. Every step from here on was completely irrelevant to me. I had signed up to do 50K and I had achieved it.

Leyla is literally carrying me over the finish line of the ultra as Jase Windu looks on. Leyla may have been smiling on the outside, but I am sure she was crying on the inside. I was sobbing on the outside and blubbering on the inside. This is what a Canadian runner's wall looks like.

I understand that it was a small event and the distances might have been a bit 'ish', but here is my argument. As a first-time ultra-runner I was told it was a 50K distance, so I trained for 50K, I visualised 50K, I lived and breathed 50K for 21 weeks. On the day, in the middle of the event, I found out it was 50K 'ish'. For a first timer that is heart breaking. Saying this, I probably should have read the Ts&Cs prior to the race; I am sure it would have mentioned that all distances were approximate or 'ish.'

Not only was it 54K in total for the race; we also had a 1K walk back to the car, making today's total distance 55K, which actually sounds cooler than 50K when I tell the story.

We had 3k left and it took a toll on me. In the time it took to finish, I will not confirm nor deny that, due to exhaustion, I almost fell into the canal, twice, or that I told Leyla and Jase I would get an Uber home after I saw 50K on the watch, while they both finished the official race, or that I crawled over the three imaginary timing mats, if anyone was around. The bottom line was that we finished it, and if you're wondering, we finished in a time of 10:29:42. A new ultra PB – for me.

We managed to walk back to the car; I managed to make it into the car; I eventually managed to make it out of the car and into a Five Guys burger restaurant, where Leyla and I had a magnificent celebratory burger. Unfortunately, Jase had other plans for the rest of the, now, early evening.

Weirdly, in the restaurant, I started to tremble involuntarily and my whole body shivered, uncontrollably; I was suddenly freezing and literally convulsing.

'Leyla, what the hell is happening to me?'

'Sean, your body is in shock. It will pass.'

I trusted Leyla to gauge the severity of the shock; it took about 45 minutes to calm down and I put on a dry shirt, which helped. Regardless of how I was feeling, I proclaimed,

'Leyla, it's not just my body that is in shock, and no it won't pass, EVER!' We clinked our hamburgers together for a job well done.

MILE 47

An Unexpected Surprise

While I was working on the computer on 6th November 2018, an email arrived that read:

'Hey Sean,

This email might seem super random but do you know the person holding the camera in this video https://www.youtube.com/watch?v=j64nQPROMMk?

I didn't even make it past the first line as it was obviously spam, or worse, a virus. I didn't click on the link and it soon joined the items in my deleted folder.

Over two months later, on 17th January 2019, an email notification appeared on my iPhone:

'Hey Sean,

This email might seem super random but do you know the person holding the camera in this video https://www.youtube.com/watch?v=j64nQPROMMk?

My company, Jukin Media, licenses videos from the internet and our team saw this and love it! We are working with the Olympics on an advertising campaign – your video is perfect for it!'

I read more than the first line this time and was intrigued. As an iPhone seemed to be immune to viruses my thumb hovered over the video link wondering which video would be revealed. Would it be advertising, porn, or even worse, would my phone be overrun with malware and all my contacts be sent a new random link?

Surprisingly, the video was me finishing the 2016 Edmonton Marathon in tears. My cousin's video of me had caught the attention of Jukin Media.

Cautiously, I came up with a reply stating that I was wondering whether this was a legitimate email, expressing my concern about my personal information, and that I didn't want to be on the radar of any third world email scams. Within minutes, Jukin Media replied with,

'We get that all the time!'

They then went on to explain their company was a trusted global leader in user-generated entertainment.

On jukinmedia.com it states:

'User-generated content (UGC) is among the most ubiquitous and abundant creative resources in the world. For nearly a decade, Jukin Media has been teaming up with entertainment, advertising, and publishing professionals to develop shows, campaigns, and stories that utilize the world's most compelling UGC videos. With a library of more than 50,000 hand-selected video clips, and the ability to discover and clear UGC videos from the broader social web, Jukin Media is a preferred UGC partner for more than 1,000 companies across the globe.

Jukin Media is owner/ operator of five of the most watched social video properties in the world. Jukin can help your brand tap into our loyal and passionate fan communities that are eager to support our sponsors and advertisers. Jukin offers opportunities for paid media and authentic, engaging branded content designed for impactful interactions with your target audience.'

With a bit of research, it became legit in my eyes and, soon, there was a whirlwind of emails with three different people from the company wanting stuff from me. The owner of the video was actually my cousin Paul, as he filmed it using his iPhone camera. First, the rights of the video had to be transferred to me. Second, my daughter was in the video so I needed to give permission for her to be in it. Third, I had to get Rene's permission. Task one and two were easy and done quickly due to electronic forms and a complimentary time zone change between England and Edmonton. However, getting Rene's permission was the tough part. I had not been in contact with him nor did I have any contact information for him. The last time I saw him was when we both crossed the finish line together, three years before. I had an article that was written for a running magazine soon after the event which had his last name in it, but that was it.

I sent Jukin the article and said I had no idea how to get Rene's permission. Within 30 minutes, an email dropped into my inbox that read,

'*We found him, and he has given his permission.*'

What the hell? How the hell? Impossible! These were the three simultaneous thoughts that went through my mind when I read the reply.

All paperwork and permissions between London, Edmonton, and myself were wrapped up within an hour – unbelievable!

The next day, the 'Try not to cry' page on Facebook had created a short video using my video and called it, 'All you need is somebody to believe in you, no matter what!' They changed my name and tweaked the actual story and added some emotional music, but then the video just took off. Notifications on my iPhone blew up with friends asking the same question,

'Is this you in this video?'

A few days later, 'The Bible Series' Facebook page also created a video, calling it 'Sometimes all we need is someone to believe in us'. This time, they used my real name but blurred out my Flash top.

During the same week the 'A.D. The Bible Continues' Facebook page posted the same video.

10 million, 12 million, 15 million views in just a few days of being posted.

Shell-shocked was an understatement; it was inconceivable that my story had been seen by so many people. It was the comments that pushed me over the edge:

'My first marathon was very similar. I was making great time but hit a wall at mile 18 and just wanted to give up and was sure I couldn't go another 8. I remember being around mile 20 and this guy in the race comes by and pushed me the last 3 miles. It's crazy how mental a race can be and how one person can make that much of a difference! Congrats to the guy finishing and thank you to the volunteer! Y'all are amazing!'

'I ain't gonna lie, I cried a little! Thankfully there are decent people left out there.'

'What a wonderful story. What a fantastic runner and a very inspirational volunteer.'

'God bless that stranger giving him that last push. Good man, young man, you got to the end. Good on you.'

'I absolutely love people like this young man. All you need is someone to believe in you. And it made me cry this morning.'

Reading them all moved me to tears, I could not believe people had been moved by my story.

At the time of writing, there were over 47 million views on 3 different Facebook pages. There might be other pages that I don't know about so the number may be higher. On occasion, I still get a random personal message from friends asking if it's me in the video.

Every single time I watch it and read the comments, I relive the finish to my marathon. I will someday be unable to run, but that special day has the potential to live on forever.

MILE 48

Selfies, Scales, Skinny Jeans, and a Sense of Well-being

At the start, in 2014, I was 18 stone or 252lbs in weight. In July of 2019 on my 49th birthday, I was 17 stone 6lbs or 246lbs. I try not to dwell on the fact I have only lost 6lbs in five years because the reality is, running has actually redesigned my body. I did fluctuate in weight over the years and I did get down to 16st 10lbs but, more importantly, I soon noticed muscles in places I never had them before. My chubby thighs became streamlined and toned; my spare tyre was still there but became smaller. I ran many miles, but I neglected an important detail that would help in losing weight, nutrition. Once again, I had forgotten six years of physical education.

If I went for a run during the day, I would always say to myself, I can now have that grabber bag of Peanut M&Ms all to myself, when they really should be shared between two people. The nights I ran, I would then have a takeaway for tea. I would run for the reward of sweets or junk food, when the reward should have been losing weight. I found that when I just ran for the epicurean delight I never lost weight, I just maintained my weight. What I also noticed was my body morphed into a sleeker me. I noticed this transformation by looking at and reflecting on all the selfies I had taken. My four chins became two, my face wasn't puffy, and you could actually see my cheekbones.

You may not believe me, but I am pretty much the same weight in these pictures, give or take 5 or 6 pounds. Now, before you email me to tell me that muscle weighs more than fat, I already know that. It's probably the only thing I do remember from my physical education degree.

It was not until a family trip to Junction 32 in Castleford and a quick stop in the Gap, where, at Wendy's request, I, with embarrassment, tried on some skinny jeans, AND THEY BLOODY FIT! With this new revelation, out went all my 42-inch waist trousers and in came 38-inch waist stretchy slim fit jeans. This was all a bit of a shock to the system as I had still only lost 6lbs.

Beyond the weight and the selfies, body confidence has ruled the day during this journey. For example, on the beach during a family trip to Ibiza in 2015, I removed my shirt without hesitation and was walking around like that in public; this would have been a huge no-no just two years earlier.

So, as I look at my wall of fame in my Man Cave and the hundreds of selfies that I've taken, I can definitely track the impact that running has had on me. It has never been about the number on the scales between my feet on a Monday morning.

This is my wall of fame, located in my Man Cave. It showcases my running accomplishments, body transformation via selfies, and, of course the medals that have been collected throughout my journey. The wall keeps me humble as it tells the story of where I was and where I am now. It inspires and motivates me to keep going every time I'm in the Cave setting up for my weekly poker league nights. I also find myself looking at that wall of fame, reflecting on my journey as I sit peacefully in my reclinable leather chair – well, at least until my wife and kids find out where I am.

I am proud of myself for my achievements, but I didn't do it alone. At the end of the day, just knowing I have run an ultra and a marathon has given me quiet confidence in other areas of my life. My running life has truly made my non-running life more fun, less stressful, and clear. It is this clarity that has enabled me to be mindful of what is important to me: family, friends, a positive work life balance, and an overall sense of well-being.

Feeling better in your skin should be the ultimate goal when you go on your own running journey, as people come in all different shapes and sizes. You need to embrace the size you are, have confidence in yourself, have confidence in your ability to make the changes you want to happen, and just having the confidence that you CAN start your journey whenever you want. If you want to finish, first you have to start.

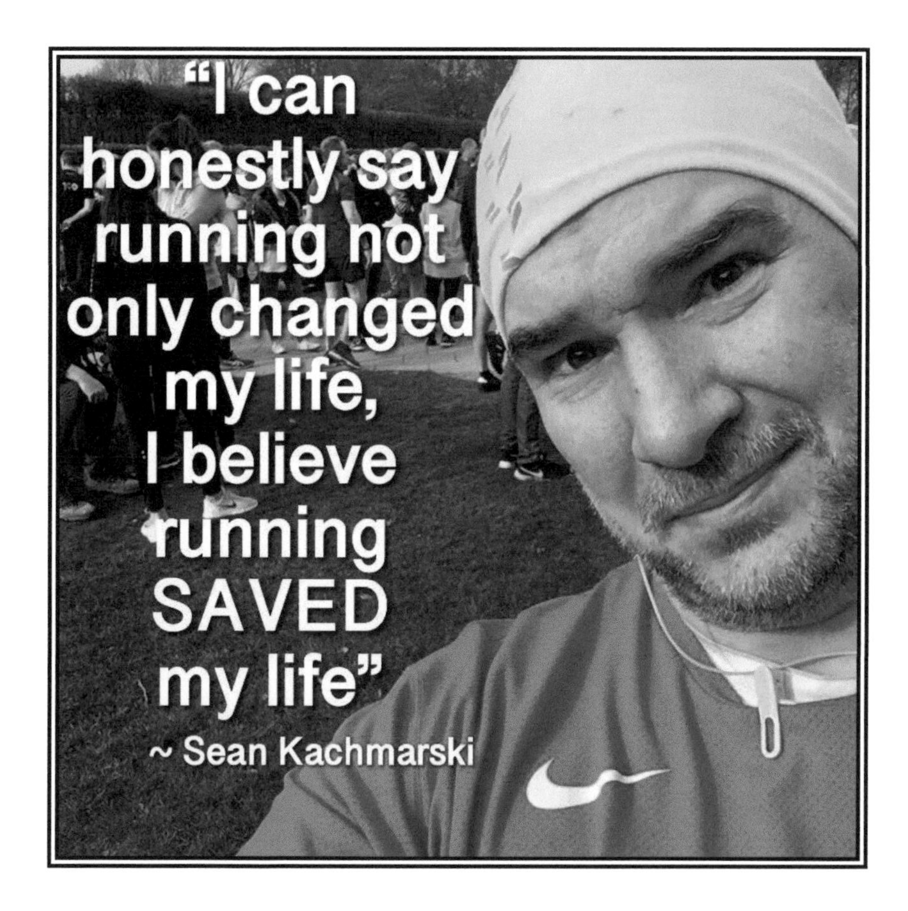

The Epilogue

To write this book, I used many of the same strategies I used during my running journey. When I decided to capture my running thoughts, feelings, and experiences in a book, I set myself a timeline of 52 weeks – one year – like a training plan displayed on my fridge. I did some research, talked to people, and got some resources together, which I could equate to the training and research aspect I followed during my running journey. Finally, I sat down to write this book; the time, motivation, frustrations, excitement, focus, anger, sadness, exhilaration, and sense of accomplishment in doing so was like running three back-to-back-to-back marathons with a 50K ultra as a cool down, without water.

When I was young, I was an overweight child who then morphed into an overweight adult. I didn't like running and to say I would become a runner would be an absurdity. Fast forward to today; I can run a 10K at the drop of a hat and maybe even a half marathon. I am now called a marathoner and an ultra-marathoner, and I now WANT to run, as opposed to needing to run for my health.

With all this being said, one of the biggest things I still struggle with as a runner, is not fully immersing myself into the running community or culture. Maybe part of me still doesn't fully consider myself a runner, as farcical as that sounds maybe it's the vulnerability I feel when exhaustion takes hold; or maybe I don't see the traits that exemplifies what a runner is, in myself. That journey continues.

When I was growing up, for me, grammar and spelling were a struggle. I was taught spelling when it was taught phonetically. As I moved out of the foundation stages of my education in Canada, phonetic spelling became the incorrect way to teach spelling. Unfortunately for me, the die had been cast. I never liked writing, nor was I any good, but my thinking was that if I could become an ultra-marathoner, I could become a writer. Like running, with lots of support from family, friends, and strangers, I wrote this book.

Visualisation is also what I used in both my running and writing journeys. Be it the finish gantry, noticing my family at the finish line, or seeing 50K on a running watch. These equate to opening the first box of your newly printed book, or seeing somebody reading your book, or seeing your book on Amazon; the strategies are the same.

Being a huge movie buff, a line from the Matrix really summed up the way I prepared for every race and for writing this book. The original quote was 'Don't think you are, know you are.' It was spoken during an epic training battle between Neo and Morpheus, in what I would call a classic dojo. In the moment, the words resonated with me, so I stole it, tweaked it, and now use it as my life motto: 'Don't think you can, know you can.'

I did get a bit of push back about using the cover photo that I chose for this book.

100 metres away from the finish of the 2016 Edmonton Marathon.

I was told this picture was 'too busy'; there were 'too many people in the picture'; and that 'you need to have 'a picture of just you'. This book may be about me, and how I became a runner, but I have realised that, based on the ancient African proverb, it takes a village to create a runner. The cover photo has so much meaning for me and I would like to share those thoughts with you, the reader: in the picture, you will see from left to right: Paul my cousin holding the camera, Jakob my nephew, Rene my running hero, Tasha my daughter, and, of course, myself, mid gulp cry. The roads were closed and the spectators had disbanded. It was taken about 100 metres before the finish of the Edmonton Marathon and if you notice, in both pictures on the front and on the back of the book, I'm covering my face. To me, this represents the isolation I felt and the realisation that my journey was never about me, it was about the others in the picture: my family, strangers, and people watching through the lens of social media. The journey you want to start or have already started, will weirdly not be about you; it will be about the strangers that helped you along the way; the new friends you make; your family who, I hope, will always be by your side; and the supporters who watch from afar through the screens on their phones. Sometimes, the road ahead will be long and empty, but trust me, you will become a better person for taking that journey. This one picture pretty much captures my entire running journey. This picture is worth a 1,000 miles.

It is very much a cliché to say, but if you really set your mind on something, you can achieve anything. I never set my mind on achieving a specific finishing time for races; that, to me, was never really that important. I would set my mind on the challenge itself and it was that specific challenge ahead that drove me. With every single race or challenge I attempted, my only goal was to finish, and it was that visualisation of me finishing that allowed me to overcome all the obstacles. With running, I achieved the impossible and I know I will achieve more in the future.

Before I started writing this book, I saw it as an insurmountable challenge; I don't even know if it will ever see the light of day, but I can rest in the solus that the challenge that drove me, was not how many books I will sell, it was to just finish my first book, which I just did.

Acknowledgments

As a fatalist, I believe that my journey was set out the minute Briony Bullard typed the words, 'Have you ever heard of parkrun?' on Facebook. If you want to think deeper, maybe the journey actually started the day I met Briony on cruise ships for the first time, way back when … who knows. All I know is there are a lot of people I must thank for all the positive emotions and friendships, the excitement of achieving personal victories; I'm even grateful for the agony of a DNF.

If there was no Briony, there may never have been parkrun; without parkrun there may have been no drive to run a full 5K, which would have led to no 10K races, no thought of running the Great North Run, and no finishing my first challenge of three half marathons in three consecutive weekends. Without that order of events, I would not have had to endure a failed attempt at the Manchester Marathon. So, in a weird way I have to thank the marshal for stopping me, because if I had actually finished the Manchester Marathon, I would not have entered the Edmonton Marathon, which led to everything else, including the writing of this book. It is weird how it all happened the way it did. If it was not for this sequence of events you would only normally see in the movies, I would not be the man I am today.

'Sean and I met back in about 2003 on the Grandeur of the Seas when we were both in our "travel the world for free" phase. We have a number of mutual friends from that contract, so upon the launch of the behemoth that is Facebook, we reconnected.

I began running in about 2010. This was when Sean was still going through his "Poker Hero" phase, which I had already been through myself (I am a croupier by trade). Sean had seen me train for, and run, the Paris marathon by April 2012 (and possibly even the NYC Marathon - Nov 2013) via Facebook and, eventually, with some gentle prodding and suggestive posts and comments, I managed to convince him that he could run a 5K and suggested "parkrun". I suppose the rest, as they say, is history as, like a lot of people who are convinced by friends that running is a "great idea", he then decided to do a 10K, a half marathon, and then a marathon (lots of gentle prodding over Facebook egging him onto the next distance each time). He's now done an ultra, which is far better than I ever did and, well, I am now waiting for the announcement that he is going to do an Ironman.

Since Sean started his running journey, I have watched from afar, here in Australia, as he has moved from poker marathons to running marathons, the highs and the lows, from the sadness and feeling of failure when getting a DNF in the Manchester marathon (despite the fact that training and turning up to the start line makes you a winner anyway), to the absolute joy of watching him cross the finish line in his hometown (and that video subsequently going viral), I have been cheering.

The power of social media is evident here as we have not seen each other since 2003, but somehow we have managed to egg each other on via the world wide web, to many levels of individual achievement and success.'
~ ***Briony Bullard***

Briony may have started me on the path of running, but it's obvious to me that Wendy, Ross, and Tasha are the life blood of this journey; they were with me during the highs and the lows, they picked me up when I was down, they gave me a literal kick out of the door. Whenever I saw them during a race, my heart filled with what I could only be described as immense love and pride about the fact they were in my life. It is at times like these that I wish I was a poet; I would be able to put into words what they truly mean to me.

Rene Wache was truly my guardian angel on 21st August 2016; for somebody to do what he did during the Edmonton Marathon showed me the true meaning of a hero. The ability to show so much self-sacrifice and generosity in terms of time and effort for a perfect stranger, should be admired by others in his life. I hope that everybody has a little Rene inside them or a Rene running beside them in their races. I know I have become a better man for meeting him and knowing him for that brief time.

What Leyla Brooke and Jase Windu endured for more than 10 and a half hours running with me during the 50K ultra, would qualify them to become a Dame and a Knight, respectfully. Having to run at that awkward pace, in between a run and a walk, for what, I bet, felt like forever, cons my incoherent droning on about why 'ish' should be stricken from the English language, and enduring my spastic wig outs over the stupidest most insignificant things. They both deserve all the success they achieve in any race or in their lives.

Putting the icing on the cake, an additional thing happened on that day, which was really cool. With every international, national, regional, or local race from a 5K to 60 miles in an Endure 24 event, Leyla had never placed or received any type of trophy or plaque for her efforts. Fatefully, on this day, not only was it my first ultra, but it was Leyla's first ever placing. Leyla won the second top woman for the event and received a second-place plaque.

The running community embraced me from the minute I showed up wet behind the ears at my first parkrun. Every single person I have met on my journey have been exceptional; their advice, banter, support, encouragement, and motivation have all been magical. I have been inspired by their selflessness and willingness to comfort perfect strangers at the beginning, middle, or end of a race.

I would like to give a shout out to all the people who not only had a profound impact on me and my running but contributed to this book:

Alice Cooper
Briony Bullard
Christopher Walker
David Lee
Hayley Stinchon
Julia Church
Rachel Norton-Warsop
Sheila O'Carroll

Some of the other people who may not have known that they, in fact, motivated me, were those who would do the most basic things, such as give me a smile or thumbs up while I was running, and a 'Go on, Sean!' at races and parkruns. People who gave me advice, people who consistently liked and commented on my inane running status updates. People who shook my hand, gave me hugs after a race, and people who volunteer at parkruns and official races are the unsung heroes of this story. There are many that I mention below taken straight from where it all began, the Locke Park Barnsley parkrun. The names were taken straight from the website. Some I officially met, some I said hi to, and some were strangers who I saw in the crowd. In their own way, they kept me focused and motivated and inspired me to keep putting one foot in front of the other:

Abbie Dagg
Andrew Hollas
Andrew Porter
Andy Bradley
Anne Middleton
Annette Spokes-Ellis
Anthony Hudson
Cath Needham
Charlotte Hallas
Claire Hartley Wilkinson
Claire Wilkinson
Colin Bowery

Darren Holland
Dave Allemby
David Needham
Diane Ford
Emma Dorman
Gareth Cooke
Gary Moore
Gav Beardshall
Ian Jessop
Jacqueline Barlow
Jill Webster
John Calvert
John Downing
John Hackelton
Jon Gratton
Jon O'Hanlon
Judith Kippax
Julie Bithell
Karen Holland
Karen Windle
Katie Lee
Kevin Johnstone
Kikki Skippers
Lindsey Shaw
Marion Wilkinson
Mark Bithell
Mark Wilcockson
Matthew Lalor
Maxine Betts
Michael Byrne
Nina Kewin
Pam Buckel
Paul Young
Peter Maurice
Ricky Green

Russell Coulson
Sarah Mann
Sarah Whiteman
Si Warsop
Stacey Cooper
Stella Taylor
Sue Kaye
Toby Campbell
Tom Sweeney
Tracy Hughes

I have been asked many times what my next challenge will be. I can say with 99.8% certainty; it will not be a marathon or an ultra. Cue eye roll; most runners say that when they have just finished a big race. The only reason it's not 100% is down to two questions that I often ask myself. First, could I have finished the marathon or ultra on my own without somebody running with me? Honest answer: I really don't know. The answer to that question might be in the pages of this book. Second, what other incredible achievements could I have accomplished if I had really tapped in and utilised the full resources of the running community? I feel I have left an enormous amount of potential behind during these last four years by not fully engaging. So, my final advice to all people new to running is to ditch the focus bubble, join a running club, and embrace the village. In doing so, you will not only accomplish a lot, you will also have loads of people to share it with.

This was my 'Just Finish' story; I would love to hear yours:

Email: just.finish.stories@gmail.com

Twitter: @Just_ _Finish